D1035394

The Social Context of Paul's Ministry

RONALD F. HOCK

The Social Context of Paul's Ministry

Tentmaking and Apostleship

ST. JOSEPH'S UNIVERSITY

BS2506.H6   STX

The social context of Paul's ministry :

3 9353 00124 5255

BS
2506
.H6

204627

FORTRESS PRESS   PHILADELPHIA

COPYRIGHT © 1980 BY FORTRESS PRESS

All rights reserved. No part of this publication may be reproduced, stored in a retrieval system, or transmitted in any form or by any means, electronic, mechanical, photocopying, recording, or otherwise, without the prior permission of the copyright owner.

Library of Congress Cataloging in Publication Data

Hock, Ronald F   1944–
  The social context of Paul's ministry.

  Bibliography: p.
  Includes index.
  1. Paul, Saint, apostle.   2. Christian saints—
Turkey—Tarsus—Biography.   3. Tarsus, Turkey—Biography.
4. Tents. I. Title.
BS2506.H6   225.9′24   79-7381
ISBN 0-8006-0577-2

7702E79   Printed in the United States of America   1-577

Contents

Preface

The subject of Paul's tentmaking was first suggested to me in 1971 by one of my professors at Yale, Abraham J. Malherbe. Since that time this subject has been very much a part of my life, serving as the topic of my dissertation, "The Working Apostle: An Examination of Paul's Means of Livelihood" (1974), as well as of several articles—"Simon the Shoemaker as an Ideal Cynic," *GRBS* 17 (1976): 41–53; "Paul's Tentmaking and the Problem of His Social Class," *JBL* 97 (1978); 555–64; and "The Workshop as a Social Setting for Paul's Missionary Preaching," *CBQ* 41 (1979) 438–50—and papers read at several regional and national meetings of the Society of Biblical Literature.

In the course of these studies I have incurred many debts, which I gladly acknowledge. I am especially grateful to Professor Malherbe for his initial guidance and continuing interest in my work, and to David Lull of the School of Theology at Claremont, who has read the entire manuscript and has provided much helpful criticism and stimulation. Portions of the manuscript were also read by colleagues at the Institute for Antiquity and Christianity in Claremont, and so my thanks to Professors Hans-Dieter Betz, now of the University of Chicago; Burton Mack, of the School of Theology at Claremont; and Edward O'Neil, of the University of Southern California.

Thanks of a different sort are due to my students at the University of Southern California and to many friends at the Diamond

Bar Congregational Church. Their interest in "the book" is appreciated. My deepest gratitude, however, is reserved for my family: my wife Carol, and my children, Jennifer and David. Their many sacrifices and constant support are deeply appreciated.

Abbreviations

ARW	*Archiv für Religionswissenschaft*
BAG	W. Bauer, W. F. Arndt, and F. W. Gingrich, *Greek-English Lexicon of the New Testament*
BFCT	Beiträge zur Förderung christlicher Theologie
BHTh	Beiträge zur historischen Theologie
Bib	*Biblica*
BZ	*Biblische Zeitschrift*
CBQ	*Catholic Biblical Quarterly*
CPh	*Classical Philology*
CW	*The Classical World*
EBib	Etudes bibliques
EstBib	*Estudios bíblicos*
ExpT	*Expository Times*
FRLANT	Forschungen zur Religion und Literatur des Alten und Neuen Testaments
G & R	*Greece and Rome*
GRBS	*Greek, Roman, and Byzantine Studies*
HDB	*Hastings Dictionary of the Bible*
HNT	Handbuch zum Neuen Testament
HNTC	Harper's New Testament Commentaries
HTR	*Harvard Theological Review*
ICC	International Critical Commentary
JAC	*Jahrbuch für Antike und Christentum*
JBL	*Journal of Biblical Literature*

JHS	*Journal of Hellenic Studies*
JJP	*The Journal of Juristic Papyrology*
JR	*Journal of Religion*
JRS	*Journal of Roman Studies*
KNT	Kommentar zum Neuen Testament, ed. T. Zahn
LCL	Loeb Classical Library
MeyerK	H. A. W. Meyer, Kritisch-exegetischer Kommentar über das Neue Testament
MNTC	Moffatt New Testament Commentary
NICNT	New International Commentary on the New Testament
NovT	*Novum Testamentum*
NTS	*New Testament Studies*
PCPhS	*Proceedings of the Cambridge Philological Society*
PG	Patrologia Graeca, ed. J. Migne
PGM	Papyri Graecae Magicae
Phoenix	*The Phoenix*
TAPA	*Transactions and Proceedings of the American Philological Association*
T & C	*Technology and Culture*
TCWA	*Transactions of the Cumberland and Westmorland Antiquarian and Archaeological Society*
TDNT	G. Kittel and G. Friedrich (eds.), *Theological Dictionary of the New Testament*
WMANT	Wissenschaftliche Monographien zum Alten und Neuen Testament
ZNW	*Zeitschrift für die neutestamentliche Wissenschaft*
ZPE	*Zeitschrift für Papyrologie und Epigraphik*
ZST	*Zeitschrift für systematische Theologie*
ZWT	*Zeitschrift für wissenschaftliche Theologie*

1

Paul and His Tentmaking

PAUL'S TENTMAKING
AND NEW SCHOLARSHIP

Paul's tentmaking has never been the subject of a book-length investigation. Indeed, apart from a few exceptions, those who discuss Paul's trade—for example, biographers of Paul, commentators on the relevant passages in Acts and in Paul's letters, and historians of early Christianity—do so only in passing, with the consequence that their statements are derivative and perfunctory. Only the discussion of the nature of tentmaking—whether it involved weaving or leatherworking—has had the semblance of debate. Otherwise, scholars are content to dispose of Paul's trade with comments that are thoroughly predictable. Thus, we are reminded again and again that Paul's having a trade was due to his following a rabbinic custom of combining study of Torah with practice of a trade; that Paul's attitude toward work in general was similarly positive, even to the point of his advocacy of a duty to work; and that Paul's attitudes are to be explained as deriving from his Jewish upbringing and as differing sharply from attitudes in the Greco-Roman milieu.

Presumably, the reason for scholars simply perpetuating this *communis opinio* is its assumed truth. In the following pages, however, serious questions will be raised about the adequacy of each aspect of this consensus. The very ease with which this consensus can be criticized—due to its unexamined dependence on deutero-Pauline sources and its facile generalizations about work in Jewish and Greco-Roman sources—suggests that the real reason for repeating the *communis opinio* is not only its assumed truth but also its fundamental irrelevance.

In other words, the lack of a thorough investigation of Paul's tentmaking is not merely an inadvertent omission by New Testament scholars but an indication that his tentmaking has only peripheral significance for their fundamental and characteristic conceptions of who Paul was and what he did. Three interpretations of Paul—those by F. C. Baur, W. Bousset, and A. Deissmann—illustrate how far on the periphery Paul's tentmaking is usually placed.

F. C. Baur's interpretation of Paul[1] is representative of the nineteenth-century tendency to view the New Testament, and Paul in particular, in the context of the history of early Christianity, especially its doctrinal developments. The perspective is thus diachronic and theological and may be called a history-of-doctrine approach (*Dogmengeschichte*). Consequently, Baur studied Paul because he was convinced of the apostle's decisive importance for the history of early Christianity. As Baur put it, an investigation of Paul would provide the answer to the central question of that history, namely, "how Christianity . . . so closely interwoven with Judaism broke loose . . . and entered on its sphere of worldwide historical importance" (1:3). The reason for Paul's importance is that he was responsible for the doctrine of universalism, the offering of salvation to Jew and Gentile alike, that allowed Christianity to break loose from the particularism of Judaism and to become a new and independent religion.

What characterizes Baur's portrayal of Paul is the conviction that Paul advanced the doctrine of universalism only against the persistent opposition of Jewish Christianity, as represented by Peter and the Jerusalem apostles generally (see esp. 1:308–9). Accordingly, for Baur, Paul was characteristically a man of theological crisis and conflict, as seen in the face-to-face confrontation between Paul and Peter at Antioch (cf. Gal. 2:11–14) and in Paul's epistolary struggles against Judaizing opponents, who had entered his churches at Galatia and Corinth (1:245–65).

Given this fundamental conception of Paul as a man engaged in theological debate, we should not be surprised to learn that Baur took little notice of Paul's tentmaking. The trade itself is never mentioned, though it is indirectly brought in when Baur discusses the controversy at Corinth over Paul's waiving of his right to support (1:269–70). In other words, the only point at which Paul's trade is even in the background is the point where it becomes relevant to Baur's conception of Paul, that is, in the context of Paul's struggle with Judaizing opponents at Corinth. Otherwise, Paul's tentmaking is of no concern whatever to Baur,[2] or to those in the tradition of *Dogmengeschichte,* such as C. von Weizsäcker.[3]

A second interpreter of Paul, W. Bousset,[4] is representative of another approach to the New Testament and to Paul in particular. This approach, which arose toward the end of the nineteenth century, views Paul and early Christianity as significantly influenced by contemporary religious movements and myths—for example, by mystery religions and gnosticism—and so tries to explain the features of the piety and theology of Paul by discerning the ways that Paul adopted and adapted the religious practices and language of his day. This approach—which is thus synchronic rather than diachronic and which is less concerned with doctrine than with religious experience, especially the experience of communal worship—is known as the history-of-religions approach *(Religionsgeschichte).*

Accordingly, Bousset studied Paul because of his importance for the developing worship life—baptism and eucharist—of the Hellenistic church. Thus it is not theological debate but cultic worship that determines Bousset's characterization of Paul. Paul's piety was shaped by his participation in the Kyrios-cult, in which the presence of Christ was experienced, and his theology was largely the product of his reflection on these cultic experiences, expressed in terms borrowed from contemporary mystery cults and gnostic myths (pp. 191, 210). In fact, so thoroughly does Bousset confine Paul to the worship setting that he is seen in no other settings. Consequently, Paul's tentmaking has no relevance for Bousset's conception of Paul, nor does it have relevance for others in the tradition of *Religionsgeschichte,* such as R. Bultmann.[5]

A third interpreter of Paul, A. Deissmann,[6] has not been selected because he represents still another approach to studying Paul, an approach different from those of Baur and Bousset; indeed, Deissmann stands clearly in the tradition of *Religionsgeschichte.* For him, too, categories like *cult* and *mysticism* are fundamental for his understanding of Paul as a *homo religiosus,* specifically as a Christ-mystic (pp. 79–81 and 113–20). The reason for Deissmann's selection is that he does not view Paul exclusively in terms of the history of religions. Paul is placed not only in a cultic context but also in his social milieu. For example, Deissmann is interested in Paul's urban perspective (pp. 71, 213, 227), in his experiences as a traveler (pp. 35–40, 62–65, 88–89, 233–37), and in many other aspects of his life, including the tentmaking which was Paul's means of financing his mission (pp. 48, 235, 237).

In fact, Deissmann's interest in Paul's tentmaking is without parallel among New Testament scholars. This interest shows itself in the suggestions that Paul may have dictated some of his letters while in his workshop and that the large letters of Paul's own handwriting (cf. Gal. 6:11) may indicate hands deformed by toil (p. 49). More significant is Deissmann's characterization of Paul as "the tentmaker from Tarsus" (pp. 6, 166), which functions to place Paul socially among the lower classes (pp. 48–49, 74, 224) and specifically in "the artisan class of the imperial age"[7] and which also functions to challenge claims that Paul was primarily a theologian and that his message was theological in an abstract and systematic sense (pp. 4–6). For Deissmann, Paul is simply a traveling tentmaker whose movements went unnoticed by the intellectuals of the day (pp. 74, 224) but whose message, expressed in metaphors taken from daily life, found a ready audience among the simple classes of the urban poor (pp. 166–76). Yet, for all his interest in Paul the tentmaker from Tarsus, Deissmann still keeps Paul the *homo religiosus* at the center of his understanding of the apostle. Pushed to the periphery, Paul's tentmaking is left uninvestigated in any significant way.

In the years since Deissmann, Paul's tentmaking has remained uninvestigated, again because New Testament scholarship has continued to be dominated by the concerns of *Dogmengeschichte* and

Religionsgeschichte. There have been changes, of course. Thus, Paul's theology is placed now almost exclusively in the context of the first-century church, so that *Dogmengeschichte* is limited to "biblical theology." Baur's conception of Paul as a man constantly engaged in theological crisis and debate is, however, still very much with us; this view is evident in the widespread interest in Paul's theology as it was developed in response to challenges from opponents at Corinth, Galatia, and elsewhere. The concern for theology, though not placed in the setting of a debate, is also apparent in attempts to construe Paul's life and theology, or Luke's presentation of Paul in Acts, in terms of *Heilsgeschichte,* that is, in terms of Paul's role in God's plan of salvation.

Religionsgeschichte has gone through even more changes. To be sure, gnosticism remains a history-of-religions option for understanding Paul (or his opponents), due to the influence of Bultmann and the discovery of gnostic texts at Nag Hammadi. Otherwise the synchronic outlook of a Bousset has been sharply reduced, so that the trend has been to look less far afield and increasingly no farther than Judaism, whether in its apocalyptic, rabbinic, or Hellenistic forms. Indeed, significant contacts between Paul and the larger Greco-Roman society, its religions or otherwise, are frequently denied; or, if contacts are acknowledged, they carry the proviso that they had been mediated to Paul through some Jewish institution such as the synagogue.

New Testament scholarship is, of course, too diverse to be so conveniently summarized, but the features of that scholarship identified here—its consuming interest in matters of *theology* and its restriction of context to the history-of-*religions* (especially Judaism)—are clearly determinative in two recent and representative studies of Paul, those of G. Bornkamm and F. F. Bruce.[8]

The point of this brief survey of scholarship has been to explain why there has been no previous book-length investigation of Paul's tentmaking. Yet there should be such a study, if only to remind us that the apostle Paul can be approached with questions other than those of the theological and history-of-religions disciplines. An investigation of Paul's tentmaking will also prove to be of intrinsic interest, and, what is more, of considerable importance to those scholars who are now attempting a social description of early Christianity.[9]

AIMS AND METHOD
OF THIS INVESTIGATION

The aims of this investigation of Paul's tentmaking need to be stated more fully. There are two. The first aim is critical, that is, to discuss and assess what has been said regarding Paul's tentmaking: whether Paul's trade involved weaving or leatherworking, whether Paul's having a trade was due to his following a rabbinic practice, and whether Paul's views on work were similar to Jewish views and divergent from Greco-Roman ones. The second and more important aim is constructive, that is, to identify and discuss as many aspects of Paul's trade as possible: his experiences as an apprentice, his skills as a leatherworker, his daily life as a traveling artisan-missionary, to name just a few.

The outcome of these several discussions will be (1) the construction of a clear and detailed portrait of Paul the tentmaker and (2) the arguing of the thesis that Paul's tentmaking, far from being at the periphery of the apostle's life, was actually central to it. As we shall see, Paul's tentmaking to a large extent defined the social context of much of his day-to-day life as an apostle of Christ and played an important part in the crisis at Corinth over his apostleship.

Chapter 2 treats subjects pertaining to Paul's tentmaking before he was an apostle. These subjects include the nature of Paul's trade, the reasons for Paul having taken up a trade, and the likely features of his apprenticeship as a craftsman.

The central chapter of the investigation, Chapter 3, treats subjects pertaining to the ways that Paul's tentmaking typically impinged on his life as an apostle of Christ. Included are Paul's travels as an artisan; his lodging and means of support; his experiences as a tentmaker, including the hours, workshops, lifestyle, and social world that made up his life as an artisan; his paraenesis regarding work; and his understanding of his trade in terms of his apostleship, at least as this understanding had developed before the criticisms of his trade were made by some people at Corinth.

Chapter 4 deals with the role played by Paul's tentmaking in the crisis at Corinth over his authority as an apostle. A survey of the means of support of philosophers and other intellectuals will provide the context for discussing Paul's defense of his tentmaking as his means of support.

Chapter 5, the final chapter, concludes with a brief summary of the features of our emerging portrait of Paul the tentmaker, and with a reiteration of the importance of taking seriously Paul's trade for any study of his life and mission.

This investigation differs from other approaches to Paul's tentmaking in two respects. On the one hand, it obviously considers many more aspects of Paul's life as an artisan-missionary. On the other hand, it discusses Paul's trade not merely in terms of a Jewish history-of-religions context, as is usually the case,[10] nor only in terms of his trade's theological relevance for the crisis at Corinth over Paul's apostleship, as is recently popular.[11] Rather, this investigation attempts to consider all aspects of Paul's tentmaking, and to do so by considering them in terms of the social and intellectual milieu of the Greek East of the early Roman Empire.[12]

One problem in carrying out these aims deserves methodological attention: the problem of evidence. The evidence regarding Paul's tentmaking is problematic in several ways. For one thing, the distinction between Pauline and deutero-Pauline sources must be maintained, with only seven letters (Romans, 1 and 2 Corinthians, Galatians, Philippians, 1 Thessalonians, and Philemon) assigned to the former category, and Acts and the other letters assigned to the latter. Once this distinction is made, it becomes clear, for example, that evidence for an unqualified positive view of work falls on the deutero-Pauline side (Acts 20:34–35; Eph. 4:28; and 2 Thess. 3:10).[13] Thus, evidence for *Paul* will be drawn only from the seven undisputed letters of Paul.

The evidence of Acts, however, is more complex, sometimes representing only a late or deutero-Pauline viewpoint and sometimes preserving early traditions about Paul's tentmaking and missionary activity in general.[14] Therefore, the evidence of Acts can be used, but only after critical judgment has been exercised in each case.

Another problem of the evidence regarding Paul's tentmaking is that, even if historically reliable, it is still scattered and sketchy. Consequently, to see Paul's trade in any clarity and perspective, we must use supplemental evidence. To this end, references to Greco-Roman sources, both literary and nonliterary, will constantly be made and related to Paul. Admittedly, a paucity of strictly contemporary evidence will require us at times to go beyond the limits of the Greek East of the early empire. In addition, scholarly treatments of work in antiquity are organized around different times and places.[15] Nevertheless, given the basic continuities in the life and work of ancient artisans, a cautious and tentative use of such evidence and of these scholarly treatments seems justified.

Therefore, the portrait of Paul the tentmaker will be derived as far as possible from New Testament evidence but supplemented with generous amounts of evidence from a wide variety of roughly contemporary, or otherwise applicable, sources. Especially helpful will be the wealth of information for social history provided by such writers as Herondas, Chariton, Lucian, and Achilles Tatius, as well as by such nonliterary documents as the apprentice contracts preserved on papyrus. In addition, we shall depend upon the valuable evidence concerning several artisans: the weaver Tryphon and the shoemakers Simon, Philiscus, Cerdon, and Micyllus. This is not to assume that Paul was simply an artisan, belonging to the working class, as Deissmann argued; rather, it is to suggest that Paul's experiences as an artisan, as a tentmaker, were often similar to those of other artisans and so can be illumined by them. So far as I know, no one—not even Deissmann—has ever recognized the relevance of artisans like these for understanding Paul and his social context. We shall also depend upon the equally valuable evidence concerning several working philosophers: Simon, Musonius Rufus, Dio Chrysostom, and Demetrius of Sunium. This is to anticipate the importance of Hellenistic moralists, especially those who were Cynics, for illuminating Paul's career as an artisan-missionary. Accordingly, this investigation tries to build upon the scholarship of A. J. Malherbe and H.-D. Betz,[16] who have demonstrated the importance of Cynicism for understanding Paul and his intellectual context.

Finally, given the several new directions taken in this investigation and the many problems associated with the evidence, we need to stress that many of the conclusions reached about Paul the tentmaker will necessarily be preliminary and tentative. In any case, it is hoped that Paul's tentmaking will never again be given just passing attention by Pauline scholars and that the social and intellectual milieu of the Greek East will become more widely recognized as an important context for understanding the life and work of the apostle.

2

A Tentmaker by Trade

Regarding the nature of his work, Paul said only that he worked with his own hands (1 Cor. 4:12: ἐργάζεσθαι ταῖς ἰδίαις χερσίν), presumably, though not necessarily, at a trade. Luke, as everyone knows, assumed this and even identified Paul as a tentmaker (Acts 18:3: σκηνοποιός). Luke was dependent here on tradition,[1] a tradition, moreover, whose historical reliability is not in doubt.[2] Still, there are problems, textual and lexical. One textual problem can be resolved easily but needs at least to be mentioned. In a few Western manuscripts (D d gig) the entire clause "For they were tentmakers by trade" is missing, due probably to an oversight.[3]

The other textual problem involves the versional renderings of σκηνοποιός, but since they are in part the result of the lexical problem, they will be treated in the context of this larger issue.[4] That is to say, the meaning of σκηνοποιός (literally, "tentmaker") is obscure. The word is rare outside this passage and others dependent on it. The versional renderings point out the difficulty. An Old Latin manuscript (h) has *lectarius* ("maker of bed cushions," usually of leather), whereas the Peshitta (syr^P) has the transliteration of the Latin *lorarius* ("maker of leather thongs," such as for bridles). The church fathers make further suggestions. Origen and Rufinus understand σκηνοποιός to mean *sutor* ("shoemaker"),[5] an understanding also found in Theodoret and Chrysostom,[6] although

20

the latter, along with Gregory of Nyssa, calls Paul a σκηνορράφος ("stitcher of tents").[7] Later church tradition made Paul a "scene-painter" (σκηνογράφος).[8]

Modern scholars have made their own suggestions about the nature of Paul's trade. One is that Paul was a weaver of tentcloth from *cilicium* (goats' hair), largely because this material was associated with his home province of Cilicia. This view was popular during the last century, though it has had supporters up to the present day.[9] It has been criticized, however, by many other scholars, most notably by T. Zahn.[10] He argues that (1) *cilicium* was used for other things and only seldom for tents, (2) Paul's connection with Cilicia and its production of *cilicium* becomes irrelevant if he moved to Jerusalem as a boy (Acts 22:3), or if he did not learn his trade until he was a student of Gamaliel in Jerusalem (Acts 22:3), and (3) a Pharisee like Paul would hardly have chosen weaving, which was a despised trade.[11]

Having rejected the view that Paul was a weaver, Zahn favors leatherworking, going back to the general thrust of the versional renderings and patristic interpretations.[12] Understanding σκηνοποιός as leatherworker does not require us to assume Paul also prepared the leather, that is, that he was a tanner, who was also despised.[13] This understanding of Paul's trade has been accepted by many scholars and is indeed the dominant view today.[14]

To identify the nature of Paul's trade as leatherworking is correct, but the difficulties patristic interpreters had in speaking precisely about his trade should keep us from being overly confident about this identification. Nevertheless, Zahn's reasons, especially the first and third, for rejecting the view of Paul's trade as weaving are cogent, and so to refrain from making any identification beyond the literal "tentmaker," as W. Bauer does,[15] is to be too cautious. Tents were usually made of leather, and leather goods were associated with Cilicia.[16] Leatherworking, then, was Paul's trade; the specialized title "tentmaker" reflects a widespread tendency among artisans to use specialized titles, even though they made more products than their titles would suggest.[17] We may thus picture Paul as making tents and other products from leather.[18]

PAUL'S APPRENTICESHIP AS
A TENTMAKER

Scholarly discussion of the nature of Paul's trade has usually also raised the related question of when Paul acquired the skills of tent-making, a question whose answer is more problematic than is often supposed. Scholars answer this question by placing Paul's learning a trade against a Jewish background. Some say that Paul learned the trade from his father, adding that his father thereby conformed to the rabbinic maxim "Whoever does not teach his son a craft teaches him to be a robber."[19] Most scholars, however, say that Paul did not learn a trade until later, until he was a student of Gamaliel (Acts 22:3), providing as their warrant the later rabbinic ideal of combining study and teaching of Torah with the practice of a trade: "Excellent is the study of Torah together with worldly occupation."[20] This is the *communis opinio,* represented by scholars from both ends of the critical spectrum. Thus G. Bornkamm says, "With Paul . . . theological training in Judaism was combined with the learning and practice of an occupation."[21] F. F. Bruce agrees: "Many rabbis practiced a trade . . . Paul scrupulously maintained this tradition as a Christian preacher."[22]

However widely and confidently expressed this view is, it is open to question at three points. First, the historicity of Paul's being educated by Gamaliel, known only from Acts 22:3, is open to question for a variety of reasons, chief among them the incongruity of a persecuting Paul having been the student of so tolerant a teacher as Gamaliel (cf. 5:34).[23] Second, even if we grant Paul's education under Gamaliel, this fact does not require that Paul's education was done with a professional goal in mind, which the rabbinic ideal of combining trade and Torah has in view. People studied Torah with teachers like Gamaliel for a variety of reasons, that is, some with professional goals and some not.[24] Not even Luke understood Paul's education as professionally oriented.[25] Consequently, the rabbinic ideal would not have been incumbent upon him.

Third, even if Paul were a professional student, the ideal of combining Torah and a trade is difficult to establish much earlier than the middle of the second century A.D., that is, long after Paul. Rabban Gamaliel's formulation of the ideal (quoted above) expresses a rabbinic self-understanding that arose only in the Usha period (A.D. 140–70), due in large part to the economic crises arising from the Jewish wars.[26] To be sure, some rabbis from the Yavnean period (A.D. 70–125) worked—for example, R. Jehoshua as a charcoal burner and Abba Saul as a day laborer[27]—and a few pre-70 Pharisees are said to have worked: Abba Hilkiah, Hillel, and Shammai.[28] But the work of these Yavnean rabbis seems to have been more a consequence of their economic status than of their rabbinic self-understanding,[29] and the traditions about the pre-70 Pharisees working turn out to be late and legendary.[30]

To sum up, the widespread view that Paul first learned and practiced his trade of tentmaking while a student of Gamaliel and so in conformity with a rabbinic ideal turns out, on examination, to be difficult to maintain. This view is highly problematic in light of several questions: whether Paul ever was a student of Gamaliel, and (if so) whether his education was undertaken for professional reasons, and (if so) whether the ideal of combining Torah and trade can be documented as early as Paul's day. Since the answer to each of these questions is likely to be negative, we must turn elsewhere to explain when and how Paul learned the trade of tentmaking.

We turn, therefore, to consider the view that Paul learned his trade from his father. As we have seen, those who hold this view also claim that Paul's father was thereby following Jewish practice. This claim, which can be easily verified,[31] should not be taken to mean, however, that the practice was distinctively Jewish. On the contrary, the practice of fathers teaching their sons the family trade was also typical of Greco-Roman society as a whole, as can be shown from the generalizations of Plato and other writers,[32] as well as from numerous specific cases. Among the latter we may note the well-known case of Socrates learning the trade of sculpture from his father Sophroniscus[33] and the lesser-known case of Tryphon, a weaver from Oxyrhynchus and a contemporary of Paul, who learned the trade from his father and who in turn taught one of his sons.[34] Of course, there were variations on this practice, so that a boy might be taught by an uncle or by a local craftsman.[35] Whatever the specifics in any one case, the evidence favors the view that

Paul learned his trade in a familial context, most likely from his father, rather than, as is usually assumed, in an educational context, that is, in response to an alleged scribal ideal of combining Torah and trade. And we should view Paul's learning a trade not solely in terms of a Pharisaic upbringing but also in terms of his larger cultural context. Paul's family may have acted in accordance with specifically Jewish prescriptions, but we need to realize that the plausibility structure for their action extended far beyond the Jewish community.

By placing Paul's learning a trade in this larger cultural context, we are able to speak more specifically about his experiences as an apprentice. Especially helpful in this regard are the several apprentices' contracts preserved on papyrus, whose typical features can be paralleled outside Roman Egypt and whose applicability to first-century Tarsus can thereby be presumed.[36] To be sure, if we assume that Paul was taught by his father, a formal apprentice's contract is not directly relevant, but the information contained therein surely reflected many of the conditions and conventions of the less formal familial apprenticeship.

At the age of thirteen, give or take a year or so, Paul would have begun his apprenticeship[37] and would have spent his days, except for Sabbaths and holidays,[38] in his father's workshop (a shop, incidentally, that may have been responsible for his family's acquisition of Roman citizenship, if, as has been suggested, the tents made there had proved useful in a Roman military campaign).[39] At any rate, Paul's apprenticeship may have lasted two—perhaps three—years,[40] in an atmosphere of strict discipline and demanding standards,[41] so that when he finished his training he was as skilled in leatherworking as his father,[42] with skills that would have been widely recognized and admired.[43]

Leatherworking[44] involved two essential tasks: *cutting* the leather, which required round-edge and straight-edge knives; and *sewing* the leather, which required various awls.[45] These tasks would have been done at a workbench, with the leatherworker sitting on a stool and bent over forward to work.[46]

With respect to tentmaking,[47] an apprentice like Paul would have learned how to cut the leather pieces so that their placement would take advantage of the natural strengths of the leather and thus best withstand strains and pulling.[48] An apprentice like Paul would have also learned how to sew these leather pieces together, using either a basting stitch, a seam stitch, or a felling stitch, the latter two being used where seams needed to be waterproof.[49]

At the conclusion of his apprenticeship Paul might have been given his own set of tools.[50] The requisite knives and awls, incidentally, would have made tentmaking an easily portable trade, a fact that helps explain Paul's eventual use of his trade as his means of support during his travels as a missionary. But to say this is to anticipate the subject of the next chapter.

3

Paul's Life
as an Artisan-Missionary

With this chapter our attention is focused on Paul's tentmaking as it related to his life as an apostle of Christ. The importance of Paul's having plied a trade during this period is suggested by the fact that tentmaking was his primary means of livelihood in the various cities on his missionary journeys. More specifically, our evidence allows us to picture Paul at work at Thessalonica (1 Thess. 2:9) and at Corinth (1 Cor. 4:12; Acts 18:3), later at Ephesus (1 Cor. 4:12;[1] Acts 19:11-12; 20:34), and once again at Corinth (2 Cor. 12:14). These passages cover the so-called second and third missionary journeys (Acts 16:1-18:22 and 18:23-21:16). But another reference, one mentioning Barnabas and Paul working (1 Cor. 9:6), presumably extends the coverage back to the so-called first missionary journey (Acts 13:1-14:25), that is, when Luke has Barnabas as Paul's missionary companion. Whether Paul worked even earlier—that is, during his first years as a missionary in Arabia and Damascus (Gal. 1:17; cf. Acts 9:19b-25) and in Syria and Cilicia (Gal. 1:21; Acts 9:30; 11:25)—is difficult to determine, due to the paucity of information about this early period, but it is not unlikely. Lastly, Acts 28:30 has been read by some scholars as implying that Luke assumed Paul also to have worked even when in custody in Rome toward the end of his life.[2] In any case, even if the facts get obscured at either end of Paul's missionary career, we are still justified in generalizing, as Paul himself does (1 Cor. 9:15-18), that it was his policy to support his missionary labors by the work of his hands (cf. 1 Cor. 4:12; 1 Thess. 2:9).[3] Accordingly, we may picture Paul plying his trade wherever he was preaching the gospel.[4]

26

It is the purpose of this chapter, therefore, to discuss in detail Paul's life as an artisan-missionary, that is, to describe the day-to-day experience that arose from this kind of life—his travel, his getting settled in a new city, his tentmaking, his missionary use of the workshop, his paraenesis on work, and his reflection on the significance of his tentmaking for his apostolic self-understanding. To be sure, few of these subjects receive more than passing reference in Paul's letters or in Acts. These few references, however, will provide a factual basis for the following reconstruction of Paul's daily life, using the parallel experiences of contemporary artisans and philosophic missionaries. Only then will Paul's daily life be seen in greater clarity and truer perspective.

PAUL THE TRAVELER

On the roads of the early empire could be found a variety of travelers: government officials, traders, pilgrims, the sick, letter-carriers, sightseers, runaway slaves, fugitives, prisoners, athletes, artisans, teachers, and students.[5] Conditions for these travelers were, as is often remarked, generally good, especially at this time.[6] Hence the mobility of a person like Paul whose travels on land and sea in Acts alone approached ten thousand miles and whose roles as a traveler included, to judge from Acts, those of official (Acts 9:2), pilgrim (20:16), and prisoner (27:1ff.). W. Ramsay has understood Paul's journey from Pamphylia to Pisdian Antioch (cf. 13:13–14) as undertaken for his health.[7] We, however, are especially interested in his travels as an apostle, that is, when he traveled in the roles of missionary and artisan.

In these roles Paul was certainly not alone. Although the evidence suggests that more students traveled to philosophers than philosophers traveled in search of students,[8] still many teachers could be found on the road. Some were even more traveled than Paul—for example, Apollonius of Tyana and Dio Chrysostom, to name just two from the early empire.[9] Others from this period, though, are quite comparable to Paul—for example, Peregrinus, whose travels covered Asia Minor, Palestine, Egypt, Italy, and Greece.[10] Artisans, too, could be found on the road.[11] Some artisans, presumably slaves, would be sent from a workshop in one city to another shop in another city.[12] Other artisans, like Paul, traveled in hopes of finding a job.[13] Still others were often on the road because they followed the army.[14]

Despite the generally good conditions, travelers like Paul still faced many delays, some because of the time expended to search for a ship, usually a cargo ship, that was headed in the desired direction and would take on passengers (cf. Acts 21:2)[15] and some because of long stopovers due to winter weather (cf. Acts 28:11 and 1 Cor. 16:6).[16] The difficulties of travel included many of the hardships listed in Paul's *peristasis*-catalogs: hunger and thirst, cold and nakedness (cf. 2 Cor. 11:27)[17] as well as many problems that were not mentioned, such as mud and dust.[18] The dangers encountered by Paul while traveling—for example, the dangers of attacks from brigands and of shipwreck (cf. 2 Cor. 11:25-26)—were quite typical.[19]

On occasion Paul traveled alone (e.g., Acts 18:1), but more often in a group, sometimes a group made up of other travelers (e.g., Acts 9:7-8) and sometimes a group made up of friends (e.g., Acts 17:14-15) or of associates like Barnabas on the first missionary journey and Silas and Timothy on the second. Even larger travel parties are sometimes to be envisioned (cf. Acts 20:4, 38; 21:16).[20]

Travel companions obviously provided greater safety,[21] but they also may have provided Paul with opportunities to engage in various intellectual pursuits. Neither Paul's letters nor Acts says so, but the experiences of other travelers, especially philosophers, make this claim thoroughly probable. For example, on a trip to Borysthenes, Dio Chrysostom was greeted some distance outside the city by some of its citizens and was engaged in discussion the rest of the way to the city.[22] Similarly, Aulus Gellius's teacher Taurus conversed with his students as they traveled to the Pythian games.[23] Other intellectual activities of travelers include a Sophist who practiced his oratory, a philosopher who wrote a letter, and several teachers who read.[24] Conversations and reading were especially frequent on sea voyages,[25] so much so that certain subjects became standard on such voyages.[26] Given, then, these intellectual pursuits of traveling teachers and students we can make an easy extrapolation to presume that Paul also used the hours and days taken up in travel for similar discussions and study.

PAUL'S LODGING
AND MEANS OF SUPPORT

Having completed a journey, Paul would have been faced with a new set of considerations, the first of which was lodging. In some cases—as, say, at Amphipolis and Apollonia (Acts 17:1)—Paul's stay would have been short, merely a stopover on a journey to a still more distant city. In these cases he and his travel companions might have found lodging at an inn and then traveled on.[27] Sometimes, however, these short stays would have been in cities where there were Christian households, and so Paul, like any discriminating traveler, would have preferred the hospitality of a Christian host—for example, that of Gaius in Corinth (Rom. 16:23) or that of Philemon in Colossae (Philem. 22)—to that offered at an inn.[28] The hospitality extended to a traveler included not only bath, board, and bed, but also provisions for the next leg of the journey.[29] One could stay up to a week without taking advantage of one's host, though three days were deemed most appropriate,[30] a convention scrupulously followed by Paul, at least according to Acts.[31]

When Paul intended to stay in a city for longer periods of time—that is, when he intended to carry on missionary activity—more permanent lodging needed to be found. Initially, of course, temporary arrangements would have to be made. For example, at Philippi Paul was lodged somewhere before staying at the house of Lydia (Acts 16:15). Precisely where he had been staying we do not know, though an inn is likely,[32] but gymnasia,[33] temples,[34] and synagogues[35] could also accommodate travelers. Wherever Paul stayed initially—and stays in inns could last for several months[36]—it seems that Paul preferred to find long-term lodging in the houses of members of his churches: Lydia's house in Philippi for an indefinite period of time (cf. Acts 16:18), Jason's house in

Thessalonica for what must have been several months (17:5-6),[37] Aquila's and Priscilla's house in Corinth for a year and a half (18:3, 11),[38] and presumably other houses elsewhere.[39]

This arrangement obviously distinguished Paul from the poorest artisans and unskilled workers of a city; they frequently had to live in the backs of their shops or even in the streets.[40] It also distinguished him from those traveling Cynics who chose, as we shall see, to live in public buildings and to support themselves by begging.[41] Paul's practice of living in Christian households should also be distinguished from the institution of hospitality. That was, as we have seen, short-term, a week at most, and Paul was no permanent guest, even though, as an apostle of Christ, he could have imposed himself on a host for extended periods of time (see 1 Thess. 2:7: ἐν βάρει εἶναι; cf. 1 Cor. 9:5-15).

Paul knew that accepting such extended hospitality really meant accepting another household institution, that of attaching oneself to a householder as his resident teacher or intellectual, with the room and board and other gifts amounting to a salary. This was an attractive arrangement, to be sure, given its reputed benefits of handsome accommodations, sumptuous dining, and luxurious travel opportunities,[42] but there were drawbacks. For one thing, from the perspective of the householder, the support of the resident teacher might entail a financial burden (βάρος), as Lucian put it in his De Mercede conductis.[43] Lucian no doubt exaggerated the burden incurred by wealthy Roman householders under this arrangement, but Paul did not. His householders, being of more modest means, could easily have been burdened by an extended stay by Paul and his companions. After all, the stay with Aquila and Priscilla lasted a year and a half (Acts 18:3, 11), and other stays—as at Philippi and Thessalonica—might have been as long or longer, had they not been cut short (cf. 16:35-40 and 17:10). Consequently, Paul, not wanting to burden anyone (1 Thess. 2:9: ἐπιβαρεῖσθαι; cf. 2 Cor. 11:9: ἀβαρής),[44] refrained from this arrangement.

Paul was able to avoid being a burden because he had a trade (1 Thess. 2:9; cf. Acts 20:34), though occasionally also by means of gifts from churches he had previously founded (2 Cor. 11:8; Phil.

4:15-18; cf. Acts 18:5).⁴⁵ Therefore, in addition to finding lodging, Paul also would have to have found work in one of the local tentmaking shops. Sometimes, of course, this latter task would be made easier if Paul could find lodging with someone who shared his trade, as happened at Corinth where Aquila, also a tentmaker,⁴⁶ took Paul in; together they lived and worked (Acts 18:3).⁴⁷ Some scholars have argued, on the analogy of Corinth, that Paul's householder in Thessalonica, Jason (17:6), was also a tentmaker.⁴⁸ This hypothesis is surely possible but not necessary, for Lydia was a merchant, a dealer in purple cloth (16:14), not a tentmaker.

The earnings from Paul's tentmaking would have gone for necessities: food, clothing, perhaps even part of his householder's rent, to judge from contemporary practice in Rome.⁴⁹ To be sure, Paul was not always able to make ends meet. Despite long hours in the workshop, he was sometimes in want (cf. 2 Cor. 11:9 and Phil. 4:12). But for a traveling teacher Paul was surprisingly self-sufficient (cf. Phil. 4:11).⁵⁰

PAUL AT WORK

Having discussed what was typically involved in Paul's traveling to and getting settled in a new city on his missionary journeys, we are now ready to discuss the typical or daily experiences of an artisan plying a trade, experiences that Paul, as a tentmaker, might also have had.

Luke's description of Paul at work in Corinth using a durative imperfect (Acts 18:3: ἠργάζοντο),⁵¹ and Paul's own statement that he worked "night and day" at Thessalonica (1 Thess. 2:9) and presumably elsewhere,⁵² remind us how much of Paul's time was spent at his trade. The expression "night and day" (νυκτὸς καὶ ἡμέρας) does not mean "through the whole night and day," which would require the accusative, but "during the night and day," which is the force of the genitive.⁵³ This expression suggests that Paul began working before sunrise and continued working through much of the day.⁵⁴ Other sources can further clarify and interpret this expression. For example, to judge from apprentices' contracts and from scattered references elsewhere, the usual workday consisted of the daylight hours only, that is, "from sunrise to sunset," as the expression went.[55] Paul's working before sunrise, therefore, was unusual; indeed, it was an indication of extraordinary industry, as is clear from the opening scene of Lucian's *Gallus,* in which the shoemaker Micyllus, accustomed to working during the day, is advised to start working before sunrise and so be assured of earning his daily bread.[56]

How much of the daylight hours Paul spent at his workbench is difficult to determine. From the evidence just cited we would expect Paul's workday to have lasted until around sunset. But according to Acts 19:9, Paul, while in Ephesus, is said to have discoursed daily in the σκολή (usually rendered "lecture hall") of Tyrannus. Moreover, according to the Western text of Acts, Paul's lectures are explicitly set between the fifth and tenth hours (that is, between 11 A.M. and 4 P.M.).[57] Even if this information is reliable, as is often claimed,[58] we still should not generalize beyond Ephesus. Rather, on the basis of 1 Thess. 2:9 we should think of Paul at work from before sunrise until sunset—save, of course, on the Sabbath.

With Paul spending so many hours in the workshop, it becomes necessary for us to know more about it.[59] A workshop (ἐργαστήριον) could be located almost anywhere. A room in an artisan's house could serve as a workshop,[60] as could a ground floor room in an apartment building, with the artisan living in an upstairs room, in a back room, or even in the back of the shop itself.[61] Or a workshop could be located in a separate building.[62] In addition, though workshops might be placed outside the city— some by necessity (e.g., stonecutters' shops near quarries) and some by popular demand (e.g., foul-smelling tanneries)[63]—most workshops would be located in or near the *agora,* or marketplace.[64] Finally, workers having the same trade tended to locate their shops in close proximity to one another, so that areas of a city might be known by the trades clustered there, such as a "cabinetmakers' street" in Athens.[65]

The size of workshops varied as much as their location. The poor but free artisan who worked alone or with one or two assistants[66] naturally required less space than those operations that employed up to one hundred slaves.[67] An average shop, if that is appropriate here, accommodated from six to a dozen or so artisans.[68] Thus, for example, Cerdon's shoemaking shop is depicted as including himself and thirteen slave assistants.[69]

To return to Paul, we find that nothing is said in Acts or in Paul's letters about the shops in which he worked on his missionary journeys. But, judging from what is said about the situation in Corinth (Acts 18:3) in light of the above discussion, we might venture to say that Paul worked, on occasion, in tentmaking shops that were part of his householder's residence (house or apartment) and that were of moderate size, large enough at least to absorb one more worker.

Looking more closely at the workshop, its furnishings and characteristic activities, we may note that some workshops, such as those of smiths and sculptors, were often noisy, dirty, and dangerous.[70] Others, such as those of weavers, required large and expensive equipment.[71] But a shoemaker's shop—that is, one quite similar to those in which Paul worked—was relatively quiet. At any rate, the shoemaker Philiscus could be busy stitching and still listen to someone reading aloud.[72] Herondas could even depict a slave in Cerdon's shop as taking frequent naps![73] A shoemaker's shop had at least a table and stool,[74] along with the knives, awls, sharpening stones, and oil and blacking for treating the leather.[75] In addition, to judge from Herondas's description of Cerdon's shop, there were also benches for customers and cases for storing the shoes that had been made.[76] The activities of these shops included not only the work itself but also the related tasks of selling the products to customers and, on occasion, of instructing an apprentice.[77] In addition, there were, at least in the quieter shops, the conversations of various people who had simply entered the shop in order to sit down and talk. Thus we can point to Socrates' many visits to Simon's workshop for philosophical conversations,[78] and the visit of the pirate Theron to a workshop in Miletus to learn of a buyer for the captured Callirhoe.[79]

The workshops in which Paul plied his trade probably shared many of these various features. In one respect, though, we can be specific. Paul's customers can be identified. Tents were used, of course, by soldiers,[80] but Paul's customers were more likely to have been civilians—persons whose occupations entailed much travel, such as the oarsmen who pitched tents for several days while their ship was in port;[81] or persons who could travel in style, such as Clitophon and his party, who set up tents on a ship bound for Alexandria,[82] and the rich who used tents, often deluxe tents, when attending one of the great festivals.[83]

The life of the artisan was in no way easy, though not as difficult as that of the unskilled worker[84] or that of miners.[85] At least artisans—so the prevailing wisdom went—could earn their daily bread, if they worked hard and long enough. Thus Dio Chrysostom, the Didache,[86] and Paul himself urge people to earn their own livings (1 Thess. 4:11-12), a sentiment echoed in the deutero-Pauline tradition (cf. Acts 20:34 and 2 Thess. 3:10).[87] Many artisans proved the moralists right.[88] Some of them (e.g., Tryphon the weaver) even rose to modest affluence and so had money to spend.[89] To others, affluence seemed likely enough that magicians could sell them workshop charms promising business, success, and wealth.[90]

And yet, many artisans were not so fortunate, as is clear, for example, from some of Lucian's characters. In the *Gallus*, Micyllus the shoemaker was dreaming of having much gold but was awakened before daylight and prodded to get started on a pair of sandals (1). The seven obols they brought allowed him to go to the baths and to buy a modest supper (22), but his earnings permitted him no more than a shabby cloak (9). In the *Cataplus,* we see him depicted as usually hungry, poorly clothed, and cold (20). Accordingly, death found him eager to lay down his knife and leather (15).

Death was no solution, however, for an artisan with a family. In the *Dialogi Meretricii,* the smith Philenus had always earned enough for himself and his family. But death brought tragedy. The sale of his tools by his widow provided for her and her daughter only for two months. After that she turned to weaving but barely made a living at it and so turned her daughter into a prostitute (6.293).

Philenus had been successful at his trade because of his reputation, which brings up the problem of competition. Those who lost out to a Philenus could either go elsewhere[91] or wish that the competition would leave, making them the sole potter, butcher, or dyer in their city.[92] In any case, as Lucian summed up the lot of most artisans, they could expect to earn their daily bread—literally that: a little bread and smoked fish—and then only by laboring and toiling from early morning until late in the day.[93]

We are now in a position to comment on Paul's life as a tentmaker. Like any artisan Paul would have worked long and hard. Thus his statements that he "worked night and day" and that his work amounted to "exhausting toil" (κόπος καὶ μόχθος: 1 Thess. 2:9; cf. 1 Cor. 4:12; 2 Cor. 11:27)—are no exaggerations. Moreover, being itinerant, Paul would not have been able to establish the reputation of a Philenus, much less the modest affluence of a Tryphon. Consequently, though his work could allow a claim of being self-sufficient (cf. Phil. 4:12), this claim could not be made without accepting considerable deprivations (Phil. 4:12; cf. 2 Cor. 11:9) and poverty (2 Cor. 6:10). Also, the *peristasis*-catalogs include hardships that were largely due to his life as an artisan: his being hungry and thirsty (1 Cor. 4:11; 2 Cor. 6:5; 11:27), cold (2 Cor. 11:27), "naked" (1 Cor. 4:11; 2 Cor. 11:27), and tired (2 Cor. 6:5; 11:27).[94] In short, of the cases cited above, Paul's life as a tentmaker seems to have been closest to that of Micyllus.

And yet, as hard as the life of a Micyllus or a Paul was, it was made even more difficult by his having to ply his trade in a social world that was highly hostile toward him. To be sure, subworlds existed, largely among the artisans themselves, in which work and workers were more favorably evaluated.[95] Nevertheless, artisans generally and Paul in particular could not avoid experiencing the hostility and contempt directed toward them by representatives of the dominant ethos. Indeed, these experiences must have been doubly difficult for Paul, who, though he shared the life of artisans, was by birth a member of the socially elite, the very circles that maintained this social world.

The chief stigma attached to the trades was that they were regarded as slavish. This objection stemmed from the fact that workshops—apart from those occupied by a poor, but free, artisan—employed virtually no one but slaves (recall Cerdon's shoemaking shop with its thirteen slave assistants).[96] In addition, the very position of many artisans, bent over for work, was deemed a slavish position,[97] which explains Cicero's famous remark that no workshop can have anything that befits a free man.[98] Consequently, a free man who took up a trade was viewed as having done something humiliating ($\tau\alpha\pi\epsilon\iota\nu\acute{o}\varsigma$).[99]

Another stigma attached to the trades was that they left no time for helping one's city or friends or for developing one's own soul.[100] Accordingly, artisans were regarded as incapable of achieving virtue,[101] or they were viewed as uneducated. The latter is demonstrated by Micyllus's characterization as uneducated ($\dot{\alpha}\pi\alpha\acute{\iota}\delta\epsilon\upsilon\tau\sigma\varsigma$),[102] by Tryphon's inability to write his own name,[103] by a sculptor's stuttering and otherwise poor speech,[104] and by tanners' and carpenters' fitness only for Cynic philosophy, because it had rejected education as a way of providing a shortcut to virtue.[105] The trades, moreover, were seen as harmful to the body, sometimes by their very strenuousness and sometimes by the opposite, that is, by their sedentary character.[106]

Still another stigma was that the trades, or at least many of them, were considered to be unnecessary, useful only to those who lived for luxury and extravagance. Catering to these people, Seneca said, were painters, marble cutters, sculptors, cooks, weavers, and carpenters; Dio Chrysostom added dyers, perfumers, hairdressers, and interior decorators.[107] Special censure was reserved for merchants, who scoured land and sea for delicacies for the table and for other costly items.[108]

Such, then, was the social world within which artisans plied their trades. Stigmatized as slavish, uneducated, and often useless, artisans, to judge from scattered references, were frequently reviled or abused,[109] often victimized,[110] seldom if ever invited to dinner,[111] never accorded status,[112] and even excluded from one Stoic utopia.[113] Paul's own statements accord well this general description. He too not only found his tentmaking to be exhausting and toilsome (1 Thess. 2:9), as we have seen, but also perceived that in taking up his trade he had thereby enslaved himself (1 Cor. 9:19) and humiliated himself (2 Cor. 11:7).[114] His trade also is to be seen as at least partially responsible for his being accorded no status (1 Cor. 4:10: $\ddot{\alpha}\tau\iota\mu\sigma\varsigma$)[115] and perhaps also as a cause of his being reviled (4:12).

The position of Paul that has emerged thus far is hardly enviable. As an apostle of Christ, Paul spent much of his time on the road and in the workshop. Traveling and plying a trade were always exhausting and were frequently painful; consequently, he could always summarize his experiences in catalogs of sufferings. Paul's travels, like those of other itinerant artisans and teachers, were often punctuated by delays, difficulties, and dangers. Once he was in a city there were days, perhaps weeks, of staying in inns before Paul found lodging in a household; and instead of simply becoming its resident intellectual, as was his apostolic right, he refused to be a financial burden and so found work making tents and other leather products in order to be self-sufficient. Making tents meant rising before dawn, toiling until sunset with leather, knives, and awls, and accepting the various social stigmas and humiliations that were part of the artisans' lot, not to mention the poverty—being cold, hungry, and poorly clothed.

To be sure, Paul's experiences as an artisan-missionary were not wholly grim. There was the stimulation of discussions with travel companions; there was the hospitality extended by various hosts and hostesses; and there was the friendship of householders who provided not only a room but on occasion also protection (Acts 17:10), work (Acts 18:3), scribes (Rom. 16:22–23), and gifts (Phil. 4:18). Even so, the overall portrait of Paul offered here is intended to contrast with that of E. A. Judge, who has pictured him as moving typically among the urban elite, whose houses served as salons for his meetings, and whose means provided him with a free flow of hospitality and gifts.[116]

PAUL'S MISSIONARY USE
OF THE WORKSHOP

The intellectual activity that was a feature of at least some workshops needs to be discussed and related to Paul's use of the workshop. At first this might seem an unlikely activity for a workshop, given, for example, Xenophon's dismissal of artisans having any knowledge of what is beautiful and good and just; their only knowledge was their technical expertise.[117] To be sure, Xenophon regularly placed the talkative Socrates in the workshops of saddlers, carpenters, smiths, painters, and sculptors,[118] but the conversations with artisans tended to cover only subjects related to their respective trades.[119] When Socrates discussed justice in a saddler's shop, his partner was not the saddler but the youth Euthydemus, who had been using the shop as a place to read.[120] Yet, according to Diogenes Laertius, Socrates' visits with Simon the shoemaker did cover subjects such as what is beautiful, good, and just.[121]

Before proceeding any further on the workshop as a social setting for intellectual activity, we must acknowledge that other social settings were used more often by Socrates, as well as by other philosophers and intellectuals. Socrates, for example, could also be found talking in the stoas and other public buildings, in the gymnasia, and in the houses of friends.[122] Of these, the gymnasia were especially important, becoming in fact the sites for several schools—Antisthenes at the Cynosarges, Plato at the Academy, and Aristotle at the Lyceum.[123] Zeno and the Stoics preferred the public buildings, especially the stoa,[124] whereas Epicurus used his house, known as the Garden.[125] One other setting, one avoided by Socrates,[126] was the household of the rich and powerful; these households, especially those of kings, attracted philosophers of many labels.[127]

In other words, intellectual activity—conversing, lecturing, teaching, reading—was carried on in a variety of social settings, with the workshop being only one of them, and a minor one at that. Indeed, apart from Socrates, the only philosophers we find in workshops are Cynics. For example, Crates can be found reading, according to an early tradition, in Philiscus's shoemaking shop;[128] in addition, his student Metrocles is mentioned as being in a smith's shop, though only to eat.[129] By the time of the early empire, Antisthenes is understood as having frequented Simon's workshop,[130] and Lucian can pair his ideal Cynic, Cyniscus, with Micyllus the shoemaker.[131] Lucian, moreover, regularly identifies Cynics as former artisans, further suggesting that Cynic philosophers and artisans were in frequent contact, presumably in the artisans' shops.[132] This inference is made likely by the fact that Plutarch was worried about philosophers being found *only* in workshops.[133] Plutarch was surely exaggerating, since philosophers at this time still used the other settings mentioned above—the gymnasia, stoa, and houses of the rich and powerful—though they were also teaching more in their own dwellings.[134] Nevertheless, Plutarch's statements allow us to assume that in Paul's day the workshop was *one* conventional social setting for intellectual activity.

An appropriate analogue to Paul, however, requires not merely the presence of philosophers in workshops but also examples of philosophers who were artisans as well and who used their shops for doing philosophy. At first, one might not expect to find any examples, given the widespread tendency among philosophers to despise the trades. Thus, there is Lucian's generalization that philosophers did not take up a trade.[135] There is also Seneca's attempt to refute the Stoic authority, Posidonius, who had argued that philosophers were responsible for artisans' technical knowledge and tools; they were developed, Seneca countered, by slaves.[136] And there are the numerous examples of artisans who, on taking up philosophy, left their trades.[137]

Nevertheless, we can still point to a handful of philosophers who were workers—for example, the Stoic Cleanthes, who, at least while a student of Zeno, worked as a water carrier and miller.[138] But special attention must be accorded Simon the shoemaker, at least as he was depicted in Cynic traditions of the early empire. For in some of the Cynic epistles Simon is portrayed as regularly discussing philosophy in his workshop, at times with the Cynic Antisthenes[139] and on other occasions with Socrates, Pericles, and numerous youths and public-minded men.[140] The importance of Simon, the artisan-philosopher, is that he is presented in these sources as an ideal Cynic, as one whose trade allowed him to embody the Cynic virtue of self-sufficiency ($αὐτάρκεια$)[141] and as one whose artisan life-style—for example, his hunger and thirst[142]—allowed him to be the true heir of Socratic-Cynic teaching.[143]

Though he was an ideal Cynic, Simon should not be assumed to have been widely followed even by Cynics, for on the one hand, in these same Cynic sources are unambiguous traces of ridicule directed toward Simon. For example, Aristippus, whose own hedonistic philosophy and life-style represent a counter-ideal,[144] is depicted as pointing out the incongruity of Simon representing a philosophy that advocated going barefoot![145] In short, the figure of Simon was a point of debate among Cynics. As a workshop philosopher he was admired by Antisthenes, who is to be seen as representing so-called strict Cynics, and mocked by Aristippus, representing the so-called hedonistic Cynics.[146]

On the other hand, Simon, the shoemaking philosopher, should not be assumed to have been widely imitated by Cynics, for their philosophy could easily be articulated in a manner hostile to their plying a trade and to the trades themselves. The simple life advocated by Cynics, for instance, could be understood as making their plying a trade unnecessary. Food, water, and bedding were already provided by the gods in edible plants, springs, and leaf-covered ground. In addition, cities provided baths and temples for washing and living quarters.[147] Begging could also furnish their daily bread.[148] Consequently, many Cynics were, as Lucian noted, *former* artisans.[149]

As to the trades themselves, Cynics could be censorious. A frequent criticism is that the trades catered only to luxury, to expensive and superfluous needs. Perfumers and chefs were easy targets,[150] but even shoemakers were included in the Cynic critique, as is clear from Aristippus's invitation to Simon to leave Athens for Syracuse and Dionysius's court, where shoes and other leather products would be greatly valued.[151] Cynics, then, could stand aloof from the economic life of the city, as shown by the following counsel: "Crates, having entered the marketplace and having seen some people selling and others buying, said: 'These people, because they do a complementary transaction with one another, deem themselves happy. But I deem myself happy because I have freed myself from both, in that I neither buy nor sell.' "[152]

Not all Cynics were so unalterably opposed to work. The ideal of Simon, the working philosopher, was at least occasionally embodied by Cynics. Demetrius of Sunium, for example, worked at least for a while as a porter.[153] More important, and better known, are Dio Chrysostom and Musonius Rufus. Dio, when exiled by

Domitian, led the life of a wandering Cynic and, according to Philostratus, worked at several menial jobs, though we are not told that he taught while doing so.[154] That is said, however, of Musonius, who when exiled by Nero to Gyara worked with his students on a farm and lectured them in the fields on sound judgment, justice, and perseverance.[155] Lastly, Philiscus the poor shoemaker was viewed as an ideal candidate for philosophy because his stitching did not distract him from listening to Crates read Aristotle's *Protrepticus*.[156]

To sum up, then, we can affirm that the workshop, including that of the shoemaker or leatherworker, was recognized as a conventional social setting for intellectual discourse, a setting, though, that was used primarily by Cynic philosophers. On occasion the philosopher was also the artisan, whose shop became known as a place to engage in philosophical discussions.

Is it likely that Paul made a comparable use of the tentmaking shops in which he worked? That is, can we suppose that Paul carried on missionary activity from these workshops? The answer, I submit, is a qualified yes. Such a use is inherently likely. It is difficult to imagine Paul *not* bringing up the subject of the gospel during discussions with fellow workers, customers, and others who entered the shops—given the relative quiet of a leatherworking shop, given the many hours that Paul spent at work, given the utter commitment of Paul to gain converts for Christ, and given the sympathy that Paul showed in other ways for Cynic traditions.[157]

Although a few scholars have suggested that Paul used the workshop for missionary purposes,[158] it must be admitted that confirming evidence is not readily available. Neither Paul nor Luke explicitly said so. Several passages may be understood, however, as implicitly speaking of such missionary activity. In Paul's only extended discussion of his missionary activity (1 Thess. 2:1–12), he spoke of working and preaching in tandem: "While working night and day in order not to burden any of you, we preached to you the gospel of God" (v. 9). This text does not *require* us to picture Paul preaching while working, though other interpretations, such as Paul working at night and preaching during the day,[159] are clearly *contrary* to the sense of the text. Paul's exhorting of the Thessalonians on an individual basis (v. 11) is also an activity that easily fits the setting of the workshop.[160]

Three passages in Acts are relevant. Paul's missionary activity in Athens is described as follows: "He discoursed regularly [διελέγετο] in the synagogue to Jews and God-fearers and in the marketplace [ἐν τῇ ἀγορᾷ] every day to all who were there" (17:17). These marketplace conversations, which led eventually to Paul's speech before the Aereopagus (vv. 19–33), may have taken place in his workshop, which would have been in or near the marketplace. But Luke seems to have had in mind the city's stoa; there, at any rate, Paul could have engaged the Stoic and Epicurean philosophers (v. 18).[161]

The second passage is 17:11, where the Beroean Jews, having heard Paul in the synagogue, examined the Scriptures daily to see if Paul had been right. Where the Scriptures were examined is not said, but the workshop is again a possibility, since synagogue-going was probably confined to Sabbaths and feast days[162] and since reading was one of the activities that went on in workshops.[163] In 19:12, the third passage, Christians are found in Paul's Ephesian workshop, though only to carry away his aprons and handkerchiefs for their healing properties.[164] In any case, these passages, even if they do not explicitly assign Paul's missionary activity to the workshop, at least *allow* for such a use of the workshop and so make plausible the claim that Paul, like some Cynic philosophers, made the workshop a social setting for his missionary efforts.

PAUL'S PARAENESIS
REGARDING WORK

We now turn to a subject that is explicitly stated in the text. Paul's missionary paraenesis included a precept on work, which we learn from 1 Thess. 4:10b–12: "We exhort you, brothers, to abound even more [in love] and to strive to live quietly, to attend to your own affairs, and *to work with your hands,* just as we had instructed you, in order that you might live in seemly fashion toward outsiders and that you might be in need of nothing" (emphasis added). Discussions of this passage have tended to focus on the issue of whether the exhortation to work was prompted by an actual problem at Thessalonica and, if so, why.[165] Few scholars doubt that there was an actual problem; they disagree only on the cause, with the majority claiming that the idleness was due to the Thessalonians' new belief in the imminence of the kingdom of God.[166] And yet this view has its problems. For one thing the appeal to eschatology is not based on the text itself. To be sure, eschatological notes surround this passage (e.g., 4:6 and 4:13-18) and eschatology formed a central theme of Paul's missionary preaching (so 1:9-10; 2:12). Consequently, some influence of eschatology probably cannot be denied here, but such influence need not be placed in the foreground.[167] It is methodologically better to understand the exhortation to work primarily in terms of what the text explicitly says.

Another difficulty with this view, especially if 2 Thessalonians is deutero-Pauline, is that idleness was not so obvious a problem at Thessalonica.[168] The precept on work was part of Paul's missionary instructions (so 1 Thess. 4:11: "just as we had instructed you"); its appearance in this letter, which is primarily paraenetic in function,[169] is to be understood as simply a reminder. The rebuttal, that idleness was a problem from the very founding of the church, has no warrant except the phenomenological argument that new religious groups tend to such behavior.[170] But with no evidence to confirm this argument for Thessalonica, it seems better to reject this view of the historical situation at Thessalonica and side with M. Dibelius, whose position is as follows: "In this letter . . . nothing points to a definite occasion for this admonition [to work]. According to 4:11 Paul repeats here earlier precepts which he had given the readers during his missionary stay, perhaps because such questions were always of pressing importance among Christian converts."[171]

With no specific occasion for the precept on work, why, it may be asked, did Paul so instruct the Thessalonians and then remind them of it in this letter? Why would this subject be of such pressing importance for Christian converts? A clue to answering these questions is found in the expressed purposes for Paul's exhortation, namely, that the Thessalonians might thereby conduct themselves in a seemly fashion (εὐσχημόνως) before non-Christians and that they might also thereby be in need (χρείαν ἔχειν) of nothing (v. 12). For Paul's exhortation and attendant reasons are reminiscent of and similar to traditions current in various Hellenistic moralists, though most notably in Dio Chrysostom.

That Paul's precept on work should be paralleled in *Greco-Roman* moralists might be surprising, given the widespread assumption that he was simply expressing here "the Jewish regard for the value of toil,"[172] a regard that is deemed impossible among Greeks and Romans.[173] Admittedly, some typical statements—for example, Cicero's idea that all artisans are engaged in vulgar trades, since no workshop can have anything liberal about it[174]— are clearly opposed to work. Yet, however typical Cicero's sentiments were,[175] they cannot be allowed to stand without having some important distinctions made about them. For example, when given a choice, a person of substance and status would hardly have chosen to take up a trade; he would have chosen rather to pursue one of the liberal arts or rhetoric or philosophy or politics.[176] But there were occasions—exile or financial need—when a trade was an option, as we see from the cases of Agathocles of Samos, who, when sharing the exile of one of his friends worked as a purple-fisher, and of Demetrius of Sunium, who, when caring for a friend in prison, worked as a porter.[177] More generally, Epictetus recommended work to those who were in financial need, as did Plutarch, both of them suggesting jobs like drawing water and door-keeping.[178]

Now if the privileged were, under certain circumstances, encouraged to work, it should not surprise us to hear of moralists encouraging those who were not privileged, that is the urban poor, to work for their living. Indeed, Dio knew of a good deal of investigation into the occupations (ἐργασίαι) and trades (τέχναι) that were or were not fit for ordinary people,[179] though, unfortunately, only Dio's own seventh oration, the *Euboicus,* preserves much of this theorizing.

This oration, which praises poverty, both rural and urban (cf. 7.9, 81, 103, and 125), is divided into two sections, the first treating the lives of the farmer, hunter, and shepherd (7.10-102), and the second, which is of greater interest to us, the lives of the urban poor (7.103-53).[180] At first Dio despaired over the lot of the urban poor, noting the high cost of living in a city (7.105-6) and the many unsuitable occupations found there, most of which derived from the city's penchant for luxury (7.106, 110). But after rejecting the impractical idea of moving the poor to the country (7.107-8) and after identifying the various kinds of unsuitable occupations and trades—those injuring the body, those catering to luxury, or those effecting unseemliness (ἀσχημοσύνη, 7.110-23)—Dio recommended that the urban poor work with their hands, that is, take up the handicrafts (χειροτέχναι, 7.124). Dio was no more specific regarding suitable occupations and trades, but elsewhere he spoke favorably of smithing, shipbuilding, and construction,[181] and, we might add, the occupations he worked at during his exile—planting, digging, and water-drawing.[182] At any rate, since working with one's hands would meet one's needs (χρεῖαι, 7.124), Dio concluded that there were "many opportunities for making a living that are neither unseemly [ἀσχήμων] nor injurious to men who are willing to work with their hands [αὐτουργεῖν]" (7.125).

When we return to Paul's precept on work in 1 Thess. 4:11-12, we note how strikingly similar his instruction was to the recommendation of Dio. Like him, Paul recommended working with one's hands (v. 11), and, like him, Paul argued that such work would allow one to live seemly (εὐσχημόνως) and to be in need (χρείαν ἔχειν) of nothing (v. 12).

Three implications of this background for the exegesis of this passage deserve mention. First, it is now clear that not *only* the second reason in verse 12—that about need—grounds Paul's precept on work, as is often claimed.[183] The first reason—that about living seemly—is also a warrant, since Paul's use of εὐσχημόνως is quasitechnical in this context.[184] Second, the extended discussion of Dio may give us an idea of what Paul's own missionary instructions on work included, instructions that were surely more detailed than the epistolary reminder in verses 11-12.

The third implication has to do with the occasions for Paul to advise his converts, who were in many cases (cf. 1 Cor. 1:26-29)[185] the urban poor, on suitable occupations and trades. We have already eliminated the specifically Christian occasion of idleness due to eschatological doctrines. Two other occasions are possible. For example, Dio regarded idleness as a problem that demanded the moralist's constant attention,[186] and when admonishing the idle, he wanted to recommend an occupation that would not simply exchange one vice for another (*Orat.* 7.109). Paul's precept on work may have been occasioned by a similar stock concern, a suggestion strengthened by the fact that two other concerns of Dio, sexual immorality (ἀκρασία) and greed (πλεονεξία),[187] were also part of Paul's missionary paraenesis (see 1 Thess. 4:3-6).

The other occasion for the moralist's advice on occupations is suggested by a typical scene in Lucian's *Somnium*. Lucian had just finished going to school when his father and friends gathered to consider Lucian's future. They decided on a trade over further education and discussed the trades, considering not only which ones would supply a living wage but also which ones would be suitable for a free man[188]—in other words, the same points as those made by Dio. Since Paul's congregations included households (cf. e.g., Acts 16:15, 32; 18:8), he may have had occasion to participate in family discussions regarding suitable occupations and to offer the advice now summarized in 1 Thess. 4:11-12. In either case, the importance of Paul's paraenesis on work is readily apparent—and without our having to suppose that his eschatological message was to blame.

One final point is that the precept on work is coupled with one on standing aloof from public affairs: "to live quietly and to attend to one's own affairs" (ἡσυχάζειν καὶ πράσσειν τὰ ἴδια, v. 11). Commentators have been hesitant to interpret this precept in political terms, preferring to view Paul's advice in terms of church affairs.[189] The language, however, is unmistakably political,[190] as withdrawal from politics is often termed "quietism" (ἡσυχία)[191] and taking part in politics is often termed "attending to public affairs" (πράσσειν τὰ κοινά)[192]—that is, paying special levies, going on embassies to Rome, entertaining the governor, and undertaking public services.[193] Withdrawal from public life was especially identified with Epicureans,[194] though in the first century this sectarian stance was adopted by many more,[195] some of whom even coupled advocacy of retirement with working with one's hands.[196] Therefore, Paul's missionary instructions—namely, to stand aloof from public life and to work at a suitable occupation—should be regarded, not as expressing a Jewish regard for the value of toil, or as arising from ecclesiological problems due to eschatology or even as representing "workshop morality,"[197] but as reflecting Paul's clear familiarity with the moral traditions of the Greco-Roman philosophers. Indeed, as Paul himself knew, these instructions, directed to the urban poor in the church at Thessalonica and presumably in similar situations elsewhere (cf. 1 Cor. 1:26–29), would have had the approval of many outside the churches, given the social realities of oligarchic policies in public affairs[198] and of economic necessity for all but the wealthiest of Paul's converts.

TENTMAKING AND PAUL'S
APOSTOLIC SELF-UNDERSTANDING

In light of Paul's policy of plying his trade on his missionary journeys, in light of his sharing the experiences of artisans (their travel, their long and laborious days in the workshop, their struggle to earn a living, their having to live in a largely hostile social world), in light of his likely use of the workshop for missionary activity, and in light of his inclusion of advice on suitable occupations and trades in his missionary teaching—in light of all these ways that Paul's tentmaking was related to his day-to-day life as an apostle of Christ, it should be readily understandable that Paul also reflected on the significance of his trade for his apostolic self-understanding. To be sure, the detailed and lengthy reflections arose only after his practice of plying a trade had been criticized by converts and rival apostles at Corinth (see 1 Cor. 9:1–19; 2 Cor. 11:7–15; 12:13–16). To these apologetic reflections we shall turn in the following chapter. For now we simply want to point out briefly that Paul's tentmaking was incorporated in his apostolic self-understanding long before the criticisms raised at Corinth.

From 1 Thessalonians it is apparent that Paul related his tentmaking to his apostleship in several ways. We have already pointed to the missionary use that Paul plausibly made of the workshop.

But two other ways can be identified. For example, given Paul's reference to his own working (2:9) as he reviews his apostleship (2:1–12), and given his reminder about the Thessalonians working with their hands (4:11), we may assume that Paul's tentmaking served a paradigmatic function for his paraenesis on work.[199] This function, which is stated explicitly in the deutero-Pauline writings (see 2 Thess. 3:8–9 and Acts 20:34–35),[200] is at least implicit in the paradigmatic function of Paul's self-description in 2:1–12[201] and in the paraenetic style in which Paul referred to his work—that is, in the phrase, "you remember" (μνημονεύετε, 2:9).[202] The paradigmatic function is also suggested by people being able to see Paul at work on their visits to the workshop. In other words, in his work as well as in other respects, Paul was a model for his congregation (cf. 1:6 and 2:14). More specifically, from the reference to work and the precept on work and their contexts, we can say that Paul's tentmaking certainly exemplified the virtue of not being a burden to others (2:9; cf. 4:12), probably expressed the love (or friendship) that he felt for his converts (2:8; cf. 4:9),[203] and perhaps even implied the political quietism that he expected of his churches (cf. 4:11).

The work of philosophers at occupations and trades was similarly paradigmatic. Musonius's farm work exemplified financial independence, as is clear from his argument that "pupils would seem to me benefitted by seeing [the philosopher] at work in the fields, demonstrating by his own labor the lessons which philosophy inculcates—that one should endure hardships, and suffer the pains of labor with his own body, rather than depend upon another for sustenance."[204]

Similarly, the Cynic Demetrius of Sunium worked as a porter in order to care for his friend in prison and thereby showed his friendship,[205] whereas Dio's various odd jobs as an exile may have been a way of keeping a low political profile.[206]

The second way that Paul understood his tentmaking in terms of his apostleship is suggested by 1 Thess. 2:4–5, where Paul regarded his divine commission to preach (cf. v. 4) as precluding any use of that commission for personal gain (cf. v. 5). As A. J. Malherbe has shown, Paul was not reacting to any accusations directed against himself but rather was dissociating himself, as any serious-minded philosopher had to do, from the many frauds who tried to pass themselves off as philosophers.[207] These frauds, stock characters in Lucian's satires, claimed, for example, to despise money but had really taken up philosophy for the money to be gained from fees or from begging.[208] The true philosopher, therefore, would have a self-understanding similar to Paul's, as is exemplified in a passage in one of the Cynic epistles: "I generally do not regard it right to make money from philosophy, and that goes for me especially, since I have taken up philosophy on account of the command of God."[209]

Such, then, are the ways that Paul reflected theologically on his tentmaking, insofar as the evidence prior to the Corinthian epistles permits us to speak.

4

Tentmaking and Apostleship: The Debate at Corinth

On his arrival in Corinth Paul found work with Aquila, whose shop provided Paul with a place to ply his trade for the whole of his eighteen-month missionary sojourn (Acts 18:3, 11; cf. 1 Cor. 4:12). On a subsequent trip to Corinth (cf. 1 Cor. 16:5; 2 Cor. 1:15-16), Paul presumably worked again, since he was proud that he had never been a burden on the church (2 Cor. 11:9). His intentions were the same for his third visit (2 Cor. 11:9; 12:13; 13:1). To be sure, on occasion Paul received provisions from Macedonian Christians (2 Cor. 11:8-9: ὀψώνιον; cf. Acts 18:5). This support, though, should not be understood as amounting to a salary,[1] nor as large enough or frequent enough to permit Paul to put down his tools.[2] Least of all should it be thought that Paul was secretive about such outside support.[3] In the main, then, we must say that Paul supported himself at Corinth, as elsewhere, by the work of his hands.

Paul's self-support was something about which *he* could boast (1 Cor. 9:15; 2 Cor. 11:10), since as an apostle he was entitled to be supported (1 Cor. 9:6-14; cf. 1 Thess. 2:7). But *others*—some from within the Corinthian church as well as some rival missionaries who entered Corinth sometime after Paul's missionary visit—criticized him for his working to support himself. So sharp were these criticisms that doubt was cast on Paul's apostleship, prompting him on several occasions to defend his practice of self-support (1 Cor. 9:1-19; 2 Cor. 11:7-15; 12:13-16).

The importance of the debate over the appropriate means of

apostolic support has, of course, been recognized by scholars deal-
ing with the many problems and the opposition that Paul con-
fronted in Corinth.[4] These scholars, however, have been hampered
in their understanding of this debate in several ways, chief among
them being the inadequacy of the background against which they
view this debate. For example, D. Georgi, H.-D. Betz, and G.
Theissen have compared Paul's (or his opponents') means of support to the Cynic practice of begging. Since Paul did not beg and
since his opponents accepted support from the Corinthians (cf. 2
Cor. 2:17; 11:12, 20), Georgi and Theissen dissociate Paul from
Cynics and compare his opponents with them.[5] Betz, however,
views Cynic begging and its consequent acceptance of poverty as a
distinguishing feature of the true philosopher and as a critique of
the wealth of false philosophers and charlatans. Since Paul's work
made him poor (cf. 2 Cor. 6:10) and since his opponents accepted
support, Betz sees Paul defending himself by adopting a Cynic
stance, presenting himself as a poor and therefore true apostle and
his opponents as avaricious and therefore false apostles.[6]

Begging, however, is simply not an adequate background in this
context. Paul obviously did not beg, and if begging is taken literally, neither did his opponents. The debate over appropriate
means of apostolic support, then, needs to be placed in a broader
context. Consequently, one task of this chapter will be to identify
the several ways that intellectuals of Paul's day—philosophers,
Sophists, teachers—supported themselves, and to point out the
principal features of the debates over these means of support.
Paul's use of his trade to support himself and the controversy his
practice engendered will then be placed against this broader
background.[7]

Furthermore, recent treatments of Paul's defense of his self-support tend to isolate Paul from his cultural context and to view the
whole matter too abstractly, that is, exclusively in terms of
theology with no consideration of the social realities involved.[8]
Consequently, a second task of this chapter will be to place Paul
within a tradition regarding his means of support and to draw attention to the sociological dimensions of the debate over Paul's
tentmaking.

PHILOSOPHERS AND THEIR
MEANS OF SUPPORT

One of the tractates of Musonius Rufus, a younger contemporary of Paul, bears the title "What Means of Support Is Appropriate for a Philosopher?"[9] Unfortunately, only a portion of this tractate has survived, so that we do not know the various options discussed by Musonius. Nevertheless, it is still clear that the means of support befitting a philosopher was a matter of debate in Paul's day. And other sources can be used to identify the various options open to philosophers and other intellectuals. In order to appreciate the variety of options and the debates over the appropriate means of support, we shall discuss four options that were open to philosophers: charging fees, entering the households of the rich and powerful, begging, and working.

The practice of charging fees ($\mu\iota\sigma\theta\omicron\iota$) was popularized by Sophists, with Protagoras of Abdera credited with taking the lead[10] and with many other Sophists—Gorgias, Hippias, Prodicus, Antiphon, Euthydemus, Evenus, and Isocrates—following suit.[11] Fees were charged either by the lecture or for a course of study,[12] and given the high fees charged by many Sophists—100 minas for a course of study under Protagoras and Gorgias[13]—we should not be surprised that many Sophists became wealthy, with Protagoras's and Gorgias's wealth becoming proverbial.[14]

The practice of charging fees was taken up by most representatives of the second sophistic movement,[15] which did not flower until the second century A.D. but whose earliest representatives go back to the time of Paul.[16] In any case, charging fees was not limited to Sophists but was also widely adopted by philosophers. Socrates, as we shall see, refused to charge fees, but Socratics like Aeschines did charge fees[17] and presumably others did too.[18] With the rise of the various philosophical schools in the fourth century, charging fees was often taken up—especially by Stoics[19] but also by Platonists and Aristotelians.[20] This means of support was still popular, therefore, in the early empire.[21]

The practice of charging fees, as popular as it was, was criticized by others, most notably by Socrates. Widely known for not charging fees,[22] Socrates, particularly in the Platonic writings, compared Sophists to traders and merchants (κάπηλοι), the comparison being made to impute to Sophists the motives of deceit and avarice.[23] This criticism of Sophists became traditional, but was also extended to philosophers too, if they charged fees or otherwise were perceived as suspect.[24]

A more substantive criticism of the practice of charging fees was that one's freedom was thereby jeopardized. As Socrates, particularly in Xenophon's writings, put it, by not charging fees he was preserving his freedom because had he charged fees he would have been compelled—compulsion being the essence of slavery—to teach anyone who had the fee.[25] Hence Socrates could boast: "What man is more free than I, who accepts neither gifts nor fee from anyone?"[26] What is more, Socrates did not need the money to be gained from fees, since he was content with little and so was self-sufficient (αὐτάρκης).[27] This Socratic argument also became traditional, especially among some Cynics.[28]

Sophists and others who charged fees defended their practice, on the one hand, by denying the charge of being greedy[29] and by pointing out that Socratic freedom and self-sufficiency really meant taking up a life no slave would endure[30] and, on the other hand, by asserting that their fees simply reflected the worth of their instruction.[31]

A second means of support—used by philosophers, rhetors, even grammar teachers—was entering the household of a king or simply that of a rich and powerful person. Entering a household, to judge from Lucian's *De Mercede conductis,* usually involved living in the patron's house, attending his banquets, and traveling with him. The responsibility of the philosopher, however, was to provide instruction for his patron's son(s) or simply to give counsel and so serve as the patron's resident intellectual. In either case, the philosopher, as part of a household, received a salary (μισθός) or gifts from his patron.[32]

The philosophers who adopted this means of support were legion. Familiar examples are Aristippus, whose stays at Dionysius's court in Syracuse will be detailed below; Plato, who also left Athens for Dionysius's court and who received over eighty talents;[33] and Aristotle, who entered the household of Philip, king of Macedon, to teach his son Alexander, for which Aristotle is reported to have received large gifts.[34] Many Platonists and Aristotelians followed suit, as did a variety of other philosophers, such as Stoics,[35] so that by the time of the early empire we can cite a number of instances and generalizations. Augustus's imperial household, for example, included about a half-dozen Greek philosophers, who acted as teachers, counselors, and diplomats.[36] More important for our purposes, however, are the examples of philosophers and other intellectuals in the houses of the well-to-do. Lucian placed the Peripatetic Cleodemus in a household with the task of teaching an eighteen-year-old boy,[37] and he depicted Platonists in general as pedagogues in the houses of the wealthy— for two talents.[38] Philostratus described the Sophist Apollonius as a member of a Macedonian household.[39] And, more generally, Epictetus, Dio Chrysostom, and Lucian depict many philosophers as frequenting the doors of the rich.[40]

These moralists were highly critical of such "philosophers," and thus we can see that this means of support was also subject to criticism. Once again we look to Socrates, who refused the invitation of Archelaus, king of Macedon, to go to his royal household.[41] This refusal was long remembered,[42] though imitated largely only by some Cynics, as is clear from several anecdotes about Diogenes[43] and from several of the Cynic epistles, one of which, ostensibly from Antisthenes to Aristippus, advised, "The philosopher is not to associate with tyrants nor to be in attendance at Sicilian tables."[44] One reason for this advice is therefore clear: entering the household of the rich and powerful meant adopting a hedonistic life-style. Thus Aristippus is depicted as provided by Dionysius with extravagant menus, the most fragrant perfumes, expensive clothes, beautiful women, and much money[45]—all for being Dionysius's resident spokesman for Socratic teaching.[46] The more ascetic of the Cynics would obviously object to this hedonism and so to this means of support. Thus Antisthenes' advice was for Aristippus to leave Dionysius's court.[47]

It was not only the hedonism that was objectionable. It was also thought slavish for philosophers to enter the households of the rich and powerful. Thus Aristippus was thought to have enslaved himself on entering Dionysius's court.[48] In *De Mercede conductis,* Lucian's entire criticism—indeed, indictment—of this means of support is stated in terms of freedom and slavery. The philosopher who entered a household was slavish in two senses. On the one hand, he thereby showed himself to be a slave to superfluity, extravagance, and pleasure (7-8). On the other hand, he subjected himself to countless indignities that no truly free man would endure (cf. 13-31);[49] these were especially frequent at banquets: being left out of the seats of honor (15), being served the poorest of food and wine (26), and being spied on by eunuchs who were protecting the patron's wife and sons (29). But the most slavish indignity was having to line up with the slaves on the first of each month and to reach out for one's salary (23). Lucian hoped that eventually the philosopher would ask himself, "What does this splendid salary amount to? Was there no other way in which I could have earned more than this and could have kept my freedom?" (30: Harmon's LCL translation).

The defense of those who supported themselves by entering the households of the rich and powerful was to mock the alleged freedom of those who did not enter a household, pointing out their hunger, cold, and disrepute,[50] and to emphasize that they had entered a household only out of the highest motives[51] and out of the deepest friendship and love for their patrons, with whom they could share everything, since friends, as the saying went, had all things in common.[52]

The third means of support was begging. Never as popular as charging fees or entering a household, begging was in fact closely identified with Cynic philosophers. Diogenes especially was depicted as a beggar; his begging from statues so as to accustom himself to refusal is particularly memorable.[53] Other Cynics also were pictured as begging: Diogenes' followers Monimus and Crates,[54] as well as Menippus[55] and many mostly nameless Cynics from the time of the early empire.[56]

Begging one's daily bread and other necessities was adopted by Cynics as a way of attacking the greed, as they perceived it, of Sophists and philosophers who became wealthy from charging fees or entering households.[57] But begging was also an especially apt means of support for people like themselves who were homeless, who did not live in a house, whether in their own or in that of a rich patron, and so had to eat, sleep, and converse in a variety of public places such as temples, baths, stoa, gymnasia, and workshops.[58] Since they were constantly out in public, Cynics could beg from everyone they met,[59] demanding a mina from spendthrifts but taking only a triobol from the prudent[60] (though Cynics were always ready to be refused).[61]

Not only was begging a difficult means of support, but it was also regarded as shameful[62] and was easily abused.[63] Consequently, some Cynics developed elaborate apologies for begging, which were usually based on the commonplace "Friends have all thing in common."[64] Other Cynics, however, simply refused to beg.[65]

The fourth means of support was working, whether at a skilled or unskilled job. We have had occasion to mention working philosophers in another context,[66] and so shall simply summarize some of that earlier discussion. Philosophers who worked to support themselves, even for short periods of time, were relatively few, with the Stoic Cleanthes, who worked as a gardener and a miller, the most frequently cited example.[67] Lesser known examples were the Platonists Menedemus and Asclepiades, who worked as millers.[68] Within their schools, however, these philosophers were clearly exceptions. More important were the Cynics Dio Chrysostom, who worked as a gardener and at other unskilled jobs,[69] and Demetrius of Sunium, who worked as a porter.[70] To be included here is also the cynicizing Stoic Musonius Rufus, who worked on a farm.[71]

The importance of these latter examples is that they are to be regarded not as isolated cases but as definite examples of an ideal Cynic philosopher, best exemplified in Socrates' companion Simon the shoemaker. In the Cynic epistles Simon is portrayed as a philosopher who regularly held philosophical conversations in his workshop, especially with Antisthenes.[72] Simon is explicitly praised for his devotion to the teaching of Socrates[73] and is presumably the self-sufficient ($\alpha\mathring{v}\tau\acute{\alpha}\rho\kappa\eta$ς) philosopher referred to in another letter of this collection.[74] In any case, such a Cynic ideal seems to be presupposed in Crates' decision to write a *Protrepticus,* or exhortation to philosophy, for Philiscus the shoemaker.[75] Other writers, especially Lucian, seem to know of this ideal.[76]

Musonius's arguments in the tractate referred to above ("What Means of Support Is Appropriate for a Philosopher?") can now be considered in some detail. All that remains of the tractate is his discussion of farming as the most suitable means of support.[77] Yet there is evidence that Musonius considered at least one other means of support as befitting a philosopher.[78] What the occupation was we do not know. But aside from what Musonius said specifically in favor of farming,[79] we can identify two principles that must have guided his judgments regarding any means of support. On the one hand, an appropriate means of support would be one in which the philosopher was not financially dependent on anyone. Indeed, Musonius went so far in defense of farming as to say that "one should endure hardships, and suffer the pains of labor with his own body, rather than depend upon another for sustenance."[80] Musonius could speak that way because he, like so many others in this debate, understood the matter of support as touching on an all-important value: the philosopher's freedom. Thus he raises the rhetorical question, "Is not the one who procures for himself the necessities of life more free (ἐλευθεριώτερος) than the one who receives them from others?"[81]

An appropriate means of support, on the other hand, would be one in which the philosopher could work and at the same time engage in philosophical instruction of students. Musonius lectured his students in the fields on self-control, justice, and endurance.[82] From what has been said it is obvious that Musonius would have rejected entering the households of the rich and powerful as an appropriate means of support for a philosopher.[83] It is also clear that farming would not have been the only appropriate form of work. To be sure, not all trades would have been acceptable, but those that allowed one to work and still engage one's mind on other subjects[84] would presumably have been considered acceptable. What these trades might be is difficult to say, but elsewhere Musonius approved of women philosophers working with their hands, presumably at weaving,[85] and we recall what Crates liked about

Philiscus the shoemaker, namely, that he could stitch his leather and still listen attentively to Crates reading a book.[86] Then, of course, there is Simon holding philosophical discussions in his shoemaking shop.[87] In other words, if not the *most* appropriate means of support, working at a trade like shoemaking would still have been *one* appropriate means of support for a philosopher, for on Musonius's own grounds shoemaking, or similar trades, would have allowed the philosopher to be self-sufficient and to engage students and others in philosophical conversation.

Musonius was aware that his views, even on farming, would prompt others to object: "What, perhaps someone might say, is it not preposterous for an educated man who is able to influence the young to the study of philosophy to work the land and to do manual labor just like a peasant?"[88] Objections were also raised against Simon the shoemaker. Indeed, to judge from the Socratic epistles, the figure of Simon was caught up in an internal debate between strict and hedonistic Cynics over the proper way to support oneself and, by implication, over the proper way to live.[89] We have already pointed to the objections of strict Cynics to Aristippus's living in extravagant fashion at Dionysius's court. But Simon was no more acceptable to hedonistic Cynics, as is clear from the ironic sarcasm of Aristippus about Simon's wisdom. In response to Simon's proud admission of his being a shoemaker and to his threat of using some leather straps for the purpose of admonishing hedonistic fools like Aristippus,[90] Aristippus grants Simon's wisdom, for a shoemaker at least, and adds with devastating humor that Simon might more profitably ply his "philosophy" by joining Aristippus in Syracuse, where leather products were more highly valued, than in Athens, with its Antisthenes and his barefoot cohorts.[91]

To sum up, we have seen that from the time of Socrates and the Sophists the subject of the philosopher's support was a matter of debate. In time four options were debated: charging fees, entering a household as its resident intellectual, begging, and working. And yet agreement on any one option was never achieved, largely because the arguments never were intended to be convincing, being either attacks on others' motives or rationalizations of one's own.

The one substantive argument, phrased in terms of freedom and slavery, was not convincing either, since the terms were too elastic. Nevertheless, philosophers clearly preferred charging fees or entering a household. Begging appealed only to homeless and shameless Cynics. Working was the least popular option, with examples, apart from an occasional Stoic like Cleanthes, clustering among so-called strict Cynics, who appear to have made Simon the shoemaker their ideal.

With this background we can now see that the debate at Corinth over Paul's means of support need not be viewed solely in terms of Cynic begging. The options sketched above are clearly a better fit for the Corinthian situation. Paul's tentmaking corresponds to one of the options, though the least popular one, and his right to be supported, a right exercised by his opponents, would seem to correspond to the option of entering a household.

DEFENDING PAUL'S APOSTLESHIP

Apart from Luke's statement that Paul worked in Corinth with fellow tentmaker Aquila (Acts 18:3), we are dependent wholly on Paul's perception of the situation in Corinth with respect to his tentmaking and the criticisms made of this means of apostolic support, first by some Corinthians and then by rival missionaries who were in Corinth. These perceptions are found primarily in three apologetic passages: 1 Cor. 9:1–19; 2 Cor. 11:7–15; and 12:13–16a. Using these passages as our basis, we shall try to reconstruct the relevant features of the Corinthian situation regarding Paul's tentmaking.

1 Corinthians 9:1–19

In 1 Cor. 2:1–5, Paul described his missionary visit to Corinth. This description is brief and focuses on his preaching; it also mentions his weakness ($\dot{\alpha}\sigma\theta\acute{\epsilon}\nu\epsilon\iota\alpha$, v. 3). What Paul referred to here is not said, though commentators have perceived a reference to his illness (cf. Gal. 4:13; 2 Cor. 12:7)[92] or to his emotional state, shaken, it is said, by the failure and loneliness that he had just experienced at Athens (cf. Acts 17:18, 13; 18:5; 1 Thess. 3:1, 7).[93] But, as Betz rightly points out in regard to 2 Cor. 10:10,[94] where again weakness and speech are paired, Paul's weakness refers less to his inner feelings than to his outer appearance in the eyes of others. According to Betz, Paul has in fact described his appearance (σχῆμα) in terms of a Socratic-Cynic *topos* in which one's appearance is consciously contrasted with the dignified, privileged, and powerful appearance of Sophists and many philosophers, for the purpose of identifying the latter as charlatans.[95]

Betz explains Paul's appropriation of this *topos* by appealing to its congruence with Paul's Christology, which in this context would mean being congruent with a Christ crucified (cf. 1 Cor. 2:2).[96] The congruence between literary *topos* and theological doctrine cannot be denied, but surely a congruence also exists between literary *topos* and Paul's own appearance. In other words, he must have appeared "weak" to others, as indeed is clear from 1 Cor. 4:10–13, where Paul said, with obvious sarcasm, that he had appeared more foolish, weak, and dishonored than all his Corinthian converts (v. 10). What made Paul appear so is identified in the following *peristasis*-catalog, which contains an explicit reference to his working at a trade (v. 12) as well as references to work-related experiences like hunger, thirst, and nakedness (v. 11).[97] In other words, Paul's weak appearance was due in part to his plying a trade. In the social world of a city like Corinth, Paul would have been a weak figure, without power, prestige, and privilege. We recall the shoemaker Micyllus, depicted by Lucian as penniless and powerless—poor, hungry, wearing an unsightly cloak, granted no status, and victimized.[98] To those of wealth and power, the appearance (σχῆμα) of the artisan was that befitting a slave (δουλοπρεπές).[99]

It is no wonder then that Paul thought it necessary to defend his practice of supporting himself by his work at a trade (1 Cor. 9:1–27) and that the dominant theme of this defense was whether he was free or slavish (vv. 1, 19). To Corinthians who, relative to Paul, appeared to be rich, wise, powerful, and respected (cf. 4:8, 10), their lowly apostle had seemed to have enslaved himself with his plying a trade (cf. 9:19).[100]

Paul's defense of his tentmaking in chapter 9 is part of a larger literary unit (8:1–11:1) in which it has a paradigmatic function: just as Paul had not exercised his right to be supported (cf. 9:6) in order not to hinder the gospel in any way (v. 12), so the Corinthians were encouraged to waive their right to eat meat offered to idols in order not to offend any weaker brothers (see esp. 8:9).[101] Nevertheless, Paul's defense also has an apologetic function, which is our concern here.

The gist of Paul's argument is as follows: He admitted that he, as an apostle, had every right not to have to work for a living (v. 6) or, more positively stated, to live from the preaching of the gospel (v. 14), that is, to enter the household of one of his converts and receive a salary (cf. v. 17: μισθός). Other apostles in Corinth had done so (v. 12a), and a variety of reasons could be cited to justify this right (vv. 7-14). Nevertheless, Paul had not and would not make use of these arguments[102] and so accept support (v. 15a; cf. v. 12b). The argument at this point (vv. 15b-18) becomes difficult to follow, but its conclusion is clear. By not accepting support Paul could affirm that he was free (ἐλεύθερος)—that is to say, he was economically dependent on no one (v. 19),[103] as he would have been had he entered a Corinthian household.

Paul's affirmation of freedom is thus an unmistakable indication that he understood the issue of apostolic support in terms of the debate among intellectuals generally over the appropriate means of support. Freedom, we recall, was a central consideration in that debate.[104] To be sure, Paul could maintain this freedom only paradoxically. He could be economically independent only by plying a slavish trade (v. 19).[105] This admission echoes the retort of philosophers who had entered a household: their critics' claims of freedom were really hollow, since they had made their claims while living in a manner that befitted only slaves.[106]

We return to verses 15-18, for they show further reflection by Paul on the relation of his tentmaking to his apostolic self-understanding. We have noted the beginnings of such reflection in 1 Thess. 2:1-12,[107] but in the face of having to defend his tentmaking to the Corinthians that relation is made more explicit. The relation between Paul's tentmaking and his self-understanding as an apostle is evident from his reference to the "necessity" (ἀνάγκη) that pressed upon him (v. 16). This was the necessity to preach the gospel (εὐαγγελίζεσθαι, v. 16).[108] Paul, however, understood his commission to preach the gospel as not allowing him any boast (καύχησις)—no matter how long he preached (v. 16).[109] What did permit boasting was Paul's preaching the gospel without exercising his right to live from the gospel (v. 15), which explains the finality of his decision to continue his tentmaking as his means of support (v. 15).[110]

In other words, in reflecting on the nature of his apostolic commission, Paul brought in the matter of his means of support. Consequently, he formulated his self-understanding as an apostle in such a way that his tentmaking was a constitutive part of it. That is, his trade allowed him to boast that he offered the gospel "free of charge" (ἀδάπανος, v. 18). This boast is both thoroughly Pauline, a boast in his "weakness" as an artisan,[111] and very much in terms of the debate over the means of support befitting the philosopher.[112] This boast, finally, was sufficient "pay" (μισθός) for Paul (v. 18).[113] Indeed, by not accepting pay for his preaching he could even entertain hopes of gaining (κερδαίνειν) more—more converts, that is (v. 19).[114]

2 Corinthians 11:7–15 and 12:13–16a

The defense of Paul's tentmaking as his means of support in 1 Corinthians apparently did not convince his critics at Corinth. At any rate, further apologies were required, made more difficult by the arrival in Corinth of certain rival missionaries who criticized Paul at a number of points, including that of his means of support.[115]

Paul's apologies—made in 2 Cor. 11:7–15 and, more briefly, in 12:13–16a—imply at least one criticism that was raised specifically by these opponents. In 11:11 and again in 12:15b, Paul had to reaffirm his love for the Corinthians. Why this was necessary is not explicitly said, though each time the reaffirmation follows an unequivocal statement to the effect that he would not accept support from the Corinthians on a forthcoming trip to Corinth (11:9–10; 12:15a). We may find the explanation by recalling the debates over the appropriate means of support for philosophers and other intellectuals. We recall that one justification for entering a household (or for begging) was the bond of friendship between philosopher and patron, with friendship being the reason for having all things in common.[116] Perhaps the opponents, basing their having received support from the Corinthians (11:20; cf. 2:17) on friendship, had argued that Paul's refusal to be supported reflected a lack of friendship, or love, on his part toward them. (That Paul knew of this commonplace is shown by Phil. 4:15, where he speaks of the Philippians sharing [κοινωνεῖν] in his support by means of gifts.) At first Paul simply dismisses the charge with the words "God knows [I love you]" (11:11). But later he seems to respond by emphasizing his role as parent and so displaying a justifiable selflessness (cf. 12:14). His spending and being spent would be analogous to a parent storing up for a child (v. 15a).[117]

Another way that these apologies seem to respond to criticisms made by Paul's opponents is the stiffening of his position regarding the appropriate means of support for an apostle. In 1 Corinthians 9 he had in principle allowed missionaries to live from the gospel; he simply took exception to this principle and supported himself. In 2 Corinthians 11, however, it seems that Paul wanted the rival missionaries to conform to his practice of self-support (v. 12).[118] If they chose not to, they would be false apostles (v. 13), merchants of the word of God (cf. 2:17: καπηλεύειν), and thus deceitful and avaricious. Paul's use of καπηλεύειν, is an unambiguous indication of his casting the debate at Corinth over the appropriate means of apostolic support in terms of the larger intellectual context sketched above.[119]

For the most part, however, Paul's apologies simply reiterate what he had said earlier in 1 Corinthians 9 (and still earlier in 1 Thess. 2). Thus, whatever the opponents had said or done regarding the matter of support, Paul would remain steadfast in his boast (2 Cor. 11:10—καύχησις; cf. 1 Cor. 9:15) as the apostle who preached the gospel of God "free of charge" (2 Cor. 11:7—δωρεάν; cf. 1 Cor. 9:18). He had not been a financial burden on the Corinthians (2 Cor. 11:9; 12:13, 16a—καταβαρεῖν; cf. 1 Thess. 2:9) and he would not be one during a forthcoming visit (2 Cor. 11:9; 12:14–15).

The costs of Paul's boast were borne by him. There was, for example, the recognition that his tentmaking, which allowed him to preach without charge, cost him considerable social esteem. His tentmaking, his supporting himself at a trade, meant that he had humiliated himself (11:7—ἐμαυτὸν ταπεινῶν). To be sure, the following verses do not mention Paul's trade, only his acceptance of "provisions" (v. 8: ὀψώνιον) from Macedonia (vv. 8–9). But, as we argued earlier, these provisions only filled up what lack there was after Paul had plied his trade.[120] Thus Paul's tentmaking must be assumed as largely responsible for his humiliation.[121] We note, for example, that Lucian deemed taking up a trade to be humiliating (ταπεινός);[122] but, we note too that, because it signified dependence, having to accept help could also be humiliating.[123] Thus Paul's acceptance of the provisions from Macedonia may also be partially responsible for his humiliation. That we are not to regard the acceptance of provisions as *alone* constituting Paul's humiliation is further suggested by his general description of himself at Corinth as being humble (ταπεινός, 2 Cor. 10:1; cf. 12:21). In any case, the social cost of Paul's self-support should not be obscured by explaining Paul's choice of ταπεινοῦν as deriving from its occurrence in the Jesus tradition.[124] Paul plied his trade (and accepted occasional gifts) in a social world where, as Paul knew, such work (and acceptance of gifts) meant slavishness and humiliation.

Another cost that Paul had to absorb, if he wanted to keep his boast, was the personal cost. Tentmaking involved wearisome toil (6:5; 11:27);[125] sleeplessness, hunger, and thirst (11:27);[126] and, in general, a life of having nothing, of being poor (6:10).[127] Such is what Paul meant when he said he would gladly spend and be physically spent (ἐκδαπανᾶσθαι) for the sake of the Corinthians' souls (12:15).[128] When the physical exhaustion and the social humiliation that came from Paul's tentmaking are kept clearly in mind, it is easy to see that his boast of offering the gospel free of charge was truly a boast in his "weakness" as an artisan.

CONCLUSION

Our purposes in this chapter have been limited. We have sought to place the Corinthian controversy over Paul's tentmaking as his apostolic means of support in the larger cultural context of discus-sions and debates regarding the appropriate means of support for a philosopher. The options we have discussed—charging fees, enter-ing the households of the rich and powerful, begging, and work-ing—and the inconclusive results reached in these debates help to explain the similar variety and debate over apostolic support in early Christianity and particularly in Corinth. Indeed, as we have seen, the Corinthian situation involved these very options: Paul *working* to support himself, and his opponents *entering the households of well-to-do Corinthians*—what E. A. Judge, we recall, assumes to have been Paul's practice.[129] In fairness to Judge, we should say that entering a household, being the more preferable option among philosophers, was probably what the Corinthians ex-pected Paul to do. His decision to ply a trade, an option seldom chosen, was thus likely to prompt resistance or criticism. More specifically, Paul's apologies of his tentmaking, and the criticisms implied therein, show the influence of the philosophers' debates over the appropriate means of support, as we have seen in Paul's choice of language: fee-salary (μισθός, 1 Cor. 9:18), freedom-slavery (9:1, 19), gaining (κερδαίνειν) converts (9:19), merchandiz-ing (καπηλεύειν) the word of God (2 Cor. 2:17), preaching the gospel free of charge (δωρεάν, 11:7), and friendship-love (11:11 and 12:15), to cite a few shared terms.

We have sought, on the other hand, to draw attention to the ex-tent to which sociological, as distinct from literary and theological, factors played a role in this controversy. A social description of Paul's experiences as a tentmaker—the toils; the hunger, thirst, and exhaustion; the poverty—helps to explain the perception of Paul's tentmaking, by the Corinthians and by Paul, as involving weakness (1 Cor. 2:3), slavishness (9:19), and humiliation (2 Cor. 11:7)—all key terms in the debate. Paul could appeal to various literary *topoi* in his apology, and he could articulate a theology of strength in weakness because his life as an artisan made them apt.

5

Conclusions

We began this investigation with a summary of the scholarly consensus regarding Paul's trade of tentmaking: that his having a trade at all was due to his taking up a rabbinic ideal of combining study of Torah with the practice of a trade; that his view of his trade was thereby positive; that he viewed work in general positively, even to the point of advocating a duty to work; and that his views are also to be compared to Jewish views rather than to Greco-Roman ones. Scholars, however, have been divided over whether Paul's tentmaking skills were those of a weaver or those of a leatherworker.

If the various arguments of this investigation are correct, it should now be clear that this consensus needs major revision in three ways. First, the one point where there has been disagreement—that is, whether Paul made tents by means of weaving or leatherworking—is a point that can be decided with high probability: Paul made tents from leather. The thesis that Paul wove tentcloth from the goats' hair (*cilicium*) of his native province should once and for all be dropped.

Secondly, the other points of the consensus have been found, under scrutiny, to be open to serious objections. For example, we have seen how difficult it is to sustain the assumption that Paul's role as artisan-missionary simply reflects a rabbinic ideal of combining Torah and trade; such a position has problems not only because of doubts about Paul's rabbinic training but also because of the likelihood that the rabbinic ideal itself arose only after the time of Paul. We have also seen that Paul's view of his trade and of work in general was not as positive as is often assumed. He was, to be sure, proud of his trade, proud that it allowed him to be economically independent or self-sufficient. Indeed, his trade was responsible for his apostolic boast that he offered the gospel free of charge. Although his trade was taken up into his apostolic self-understanding, it was also the source of much personal hardship and social humiliation. His boast, it turned out, was a boast in his weakness as an artisan. Consequently, Paul viewed his working at a trade none too positively as toil, slavery, and humiliation. Nor was his view of work in general so positive as to amount to a duty to work, once we distinguish between Pauline and deutero-Pauline sources and discover the duty to work only in the latter. Nor was his view of work as Jewish as is often assumed. Indeed, we have argued that Paul's view—that one's occupation or trade should be seemly and should meet one's needs—was the same as the moral reflection of Greco-Roman philosophers like Dio Chrysostom.

The third, and most important, way that the consensus on Paul's tentmaking needs revision is simply for us to go beyond it, to ask more questions about his trade and how it impinged on his life, both before and especially after his call to preach the gospel. And when we ask these questions—about his apprenticeship, about his skills as a leatherworker, about his typical or day-to-day experiences as an artisan, about the crisis over his tentmaking at Corinth—we begin to realize that, far from being at the periphery of his life, Paul's tentmaking was actually central to it. More than any of us has supposed, Paul was *Paul the Tentmaker*. His trade occupied much of his time—from the years of his apprenticeship through the years of his life as a missionary of Christ, from before daylight through most of the day. Consequently, his trade in large measure determined his daily experiences and his social status. His life was very much that of the workshop—of artisan-friends like Aquila, Barnabas, and perhaps Jason; of leather, knives, and awls; of wearying toil; of being bent over a workbench like a slave and of working side by side with slaves; of thereby being perceived by others and by himself as slavish and humiliated; of suffering the artisans' lack of status and so being reviled and abused.

Paul's trade also provided him with his principal means of

livelihood, though never with enough to make him anything but a poor man and sometimes not even with that much, so that hunger and thirst and cold were at times his lot. His trade also may have served directly in his missionary activities in the sense that workshop conversations with fellow workers, customers, or those who stopped by might easily have turned into occasions for informal evangelization. Finally, his trade was taken up into his apostolic self-understanding, so much so that, when criticized for plying his trade, he came to understand himself as the apostle who offered the gospel free of charge.

In other words, despite our penchant for confining Paul to the history of theology or the history of religions, our investigation of Paul's tentmaking has made us recognize that he also belongs to social and intellectual history. Socially, Paul's plying a trade means that he shared many of the experiences of artisans, and so the evidence about Tryphon, Cerdon, Philiscus, Micyllus, and other artisans has helped us to confirm, clarify, and complement our evidence about Paul's daily life. Intellectually, his plying a trade means that he came into contact with a tradition of philosophy—in large part Cynic—that addressed itself to the question of suitable occupations and trades for the urban poor, that made the workshop one of its settings for doing philosophy, and that in the figure of Simon the shoemaker made the artisan-philosopher the embodiment of its ideals of self-sufficiency and freedom. Consequently, philosophers like Dio Chrysostom are important for Paul's intellectual background. In sum, by placing Paul in the workshop—that is, by taking seriously the fact that Paul was a tentmaker—we have located him more precisely in the social and intellectual milieu of the urban centers of the Greek East of the early empire.

Notes

CHAPTER 1

1. See F. C. Baur, *Paul the Apostle of Jesus Christ: His Life and Work, His Epistles and Doctrine,* 2 vols. (London: Williams & Norgate, 1876). References to volumes and pages of this work will be given in parentheses in the text.

2. It should be said that another reason for Paul's tentmaking being at the periphery of Baur's view is that he considers only Romans, 1 and 2 Corinthians, and Galatians to be the authentic letters of Paul. With the sources so restricted, much of the evidence—in Acts and 1 Thessalonians—is left out of consideration. In fact, even in Baur's highly skeptical discussion of the narrative in Acts (1:15–24), the reference to Paul's tentmaking in Acts 18:3 is not discussed, because Baur passes over the entire narrative at this point (18:1–23).

3. See C. von Weizsäcker, *The Apostolic Age of the Christian Church,* 2 vols. (London: Williams & Norgate, 1897). Weizsäcker's critical discussion of the Acts narrative and Paul's letters is more thorough than Baur's, so comments on Paul's tentmaking and practice of self-support are more frequent (see 1:288, 301, 307, 333, 343, 357), but since Weizsäcker's main concern is doctrinal developments in early Christianity, the comments about Paul's work are neither lengthy nor detailed. On the *dogmengeschichtliche* tradition in New Testament studies, see W. G. Kümmel, *The New Testament: The History of the Investigation of Its Problems* (Nashville: Abingdon, 1972), pp. 120–205, esp. pp. 167–75.

4. See W. Bousset, *Kyrios Christos: A History of the Belief in Christ from the Beginnings of Christianity to Irenaeus* (Nashville: Abingdon, 1970), pp. 153–210. Page references to this work will be given in parentheses in the text.

5. See, e.g., R. Bultmann, *Theology of the New Testament,* 2 vols. (New York: Scribner's 1951–55), 1:185–352. Bultmann accepted Bousset's

placement of Paul in the context of worship and his identification of
gnosticism as Paul's history-of-religions background; Bultmann then went
further by analyzing the cult's Christ-myth in terms of its specifically
Christian understanding of existence. Thus Bultmann, like Bousset, saw
Paul's theologizing as prompted more by the typical experiences of Christians at worship than by the specific objections made against Paul by his
various opponents, as is the case of Pauline scholars today. On the
religionsgeschichtliche tradition in New Testament studies, see Kümmel,
New Testament, pp. 206–80.

6. See A. Deissmann, *Paul: A Study in Social and Religious History,*
2d ed. (London: Hodder & Stoughton, 1926). Page references to this book
will be given in parentheses in the text.

7. This phrase is taken from another of Deissmann's books, *Light from
the Ancient East,* 4th ed. (London: Hodder & Stoughton, 1927), p. 314.

8. See G. Bornkamm, *Paul* (New York: Harper & Row, 1971), and F. F.
Bruce, *Paul: Apostle of the Heart Set Free* (Grand Rapids: Eerdmans,
1977).

9. For a survey of recent scholarship, see A. J. Malherbe, *Social Aspects
of Early Christianity* (Baton Rouge: Louisiana State University, 1977).

10. In addition to general works on Paul and commentaries on the rele-
vant passages (esp. Acts 18.3; 1 Cor. 4:12; and 1 Thess. 4:11), see F.
Hauck, *Die Stellung des Urchristentums zu Arbeit und Geld,* BFCT 2,3
(Gütersloh: Bertelsmann, 1921), pp. 102–11; H. Holzapfel, *Die sittliche
Wertung der körperlichen Arbeit im christlichen Altertum* (Würzburg:
Rita, 1941), pp. 41–46; A. T. Geoghegan, *The Attitude towards Labor in
Early Christianity and Ancient Culture* (Washington, D.C.: Catholic
University of America, 1945), pp. 108–21; W. Bienert, *Die Arbeit nach der
Lehre der Bibel: Eine Grundlegung evangelischer Sozialethik* (Stuttgart:
Evangelisches Verlagswerk GMBH, 1954), pp. 299–378; and G. Agrell,
*Work, Toil and Sustenance: An Examination of the View of Work in the
New Testament, Taking into Consideration Views Found in Old Testa-
ment, Intertestamental and Early Rabbinic Writings* (Lund:
Verbum-Håkan Ohlssons, 1976), pp. 95–115.

11. See, e.g., D. Georgi, *Die Gegner des Paulus im 2. Korintherbrief:
Studien zum religiösen Propaganda in der Spätantike,* WMANT 11
(Neukirchen-Vluyn: Neukirchener, 1964), pp. 234–41; G. Dautzenberg,
"Der Verzicht auf das apostolische Unterhaltsrecht: Eine exegetische
Untersuchung zu 1 Kor 9," *Bib* 50 (1969): 212–32; D. L. Dungan, *The Sayings
of Jesus in the Churches of Paul: The Use of the Synoptic Tradition in the
Regulation of Early Church Life* (Philadelphia: Fortress, 1971), pp. 3–40;
H.-D. Betz, *Der Apostel Paulus und die sokratische Tradition: Eine ex-
egetische Untersuchung zu seiner "Apologie" 2 Korinther 10–13,* BHTh
45 (Tübingen: Mohr, 1972), pp. 100–117; and G. Theissen, "Legitimation

und Lebensunterhalt: Ein Beitrag zur Soziologie urchristlicher Missionare," *NTS* 21 (1975): 192-221.

12. This investigation is thus indebted to the excellent programmatic essay of E. A. Judge, "St. Paul and Classical Society," *JAC* 15 (1972): 19-36. Judge, an ancient historian, proposes that "the main interests and events of the New Testament itself are to be seen in relation to their full context in the society of its own times" (p. 24). For Paul that means relating him to what was going on in the Greek East of the first century with respect to relations with Rome; Roman citizenship; Roman law; the life of Greek cities, their institutions and social order; education; language; literature, especially the fashion of Atticizing; philosophy; and ethics. Judge does not mention Paul's tentmaking, but this investigation is indebted to his overall approach. For discussion and assessment of this and other writings by Judge, see Malherbe, *Social Aspects,* pp. 45-57 and passim.

13. The importance of the Pauline/deutero-Pauline distinction has finally been made by Agrell, *Work,* p. 2. He thus concludes (pp. 104, 115) that Paul's view of work was negative, or at least ambivalent—a break with the *communis opinio.* The deutero-Pauline materials are capably treated by Agrell (pp. 116-49).

14. That conditions were favorable for the early formation of traditions about Paul and his churches is argued by J. Jervell, *Luke and the People of God* (Minneapolis: Augsburg, 1972), pp. 19-39. See further W. G. Kümmel, *Introduction to the New Testament* (Nashville: Abingdon, 1975), pp. 174-87.

15. On this problem in the use of scholarly literature from cognate disciplines like ancient history, ancient philosophy, and classics, see Judge, "St. Paul and Classical Society," pp. 21-22. This problem is evident in the most recent study of work in antiquity, namely, A. Burford's *Craftsmen in Greek and Roman Society* (London: Thames & Hudson, 1972). Her treatment of the Greek craftsman is better than that of the Roman, and her focus is on classical Athens and on other cities of the early Hellenistic period. (cf. the review by J. Packer in *T & C* 17 [1976]: 537-41). In addition, because of her selection of examples, the trade most relevant for Paul—leatherworking—has been slighted. Consequently, we must turn on occasion to other studies: H. Blümner, *Technologie und Terminologie der Gewerbe und Künste bei Griechen und Römern,* 4 vols., 2d ed. of vol. 1 only (Leipzig and Berlin: Teubner, 1912), 1:273-92; R. J. Forbes, *Studies in Ancient Technology,* 9 vols. (Leiden: Brill, 1957), 5:45-77; and esp. O. Lau, "Schuster und Schusterhandwerk in der griechisch-römischen Literatur und Kunst" (diss., Bonn, 1967). Other excellent, though more general, studies are those of M. I. Finley, *The Ancient Economy* (Berkeley: University of California, 1973), and R. Mac-

Mullen, *Roman Social Relations 50 B.C. to A.D. 284* (New Haven: Yale, 1974). Cf. also the detailed essays by J. A. O. Larsen (Roman Greece) and T. R. S. Broughton (Roman Asia) in *An Economic Survey of Ancient Rome,* 6 vols., ed. T. Frank (Baltimore: Johns Hopkins, 1938), 5:259-498, 499-916.

16. See esp. A. J. Malherbe, "Gentle as a Nurse: The Cynic Background of 1 Thess. 2," *NovT* 12 (1970): 203-17, and Betz, *Apostel Paulus.*

CHAPTER 2

1. So C. Burchard, *Der dreizehnte Zeuge: Traditions- und kompositions-geschichtliche Untersuchungen zu Lukas' Darstellung der Früzeit des Paulus,* FRLANT 103 (Göttingen: Vandenhoeck & Ruprecht, 1970), p. 39.

2. See E. Haenchen, *The Acts of the Apostles: A Commentary* (Philadelphia: Westminster, 1971), p. 538.

3. For details, see C. S. C. Williams, *Alterations to the Text of the Synoptic Gospels and Acts* (Oxford: Blackwell, 1951), p. 76.

4. See esp. T. Zahn, *Die Apostelgeschichte des Lukas,* KNT 5, 2d ed. (Leipzig and Erlangen: Deichert, 1921), p. 632, n. 10.

5. See Origen *In Ep. ad Rom, Hom.* 16.3 (PG 14:1279).

6. See Theodoret *De graec. aff. curat.* 5 (PG 83:945B), and Chrysostom *In Ep. 2 ad Tim, Hom.* 4.2 (PG 62:622).

7. See Chrysostom *In Ep. 1 ad Cor, Hom.* 20.5-6 (PG 61:168), and Gregory of Nyssa *ep.* 17 (PG 46:1061B). For patristic interpretations, see further R. Silva, "Eran, pues, de oficio, fabricantes de tiendas," *EstBib* 24 (1965): 123-34, esp. 124-26.

8. See further E. Nestle, "St. Paul's Handicraft (Acts 18:3)," *JBL* 11 (1892): 205-6.

9. Among those who hold this view are: E. Plumptre, "St. Paul as a Man of Business," *Expositor* 1 (1875): 259-66, esp. 260; H. Alford, *The Greek Testament,* 4 vols. (Cambridge: Deighton & Bell, 1880), 3:257; J. B. Lightfoot, *Notes on the Epistles of Paul* (London: Macmillan, 1895), p. 27; A. Deissmann, *Paul: A Study in Social and Religious History* (New York: Hodder & Stoughton, 1926), pp. 48-50; M. Dibelius, *An die Thessalonicher I-II, an die Philipper,* HNT 11, 3d ed. (Tübingen: Mohr, 1937), p. 7; W. Bienert, *Die Arbeit nach der Lehre der Bibel* (Stuttgart: Evangelisches Verlagswerk GMBH, 1954), p. 307; and F. F. Bruce, *Paul: Apostle of the Heart Set Free* (Grand Rapids: Eerdmans, 1977), p. 36. For the view that Paul wove tent cloth from linen, see, e.g., G. Heinrici, "Zur Geschichte der Anfänge paulinischer Gemeinden," *ZWT* 20 (1877): 89-129, esp. 94-95, and G. Theissen, "Soziale Schichtung in der korin-

thischen Gemeinde," *ZNW* 65 (1974): 232-72, esp. 267. Cf. further Silva, "Fabricantes de tiendas," pp. 129-32.

10. Zahn, *Apostelgeschichte,* pp. 633-34.

11. See J. Jeremias, "Zöllner und Sünder," *ZNW* 30 (1931): 293-300, esp. 299.

12. Zahn, *Apostelgeschichte,* p. 634.

13. See Jeremias, "Zöllner," pp. 296-99. For Greco-Roman society generally, see R. MacMullen, *Roman Social Relations 50 B.C. to A.D. 284* (New Haven: Yale, 1974), pp. 70-71, and esp. O. Lau, "Schuster und Schusterhandwerk in der griechisch-römischen Literatur und Kunst," (diss., Bonn, 1967), pp. 53-60.

14. Among those who hold this view are E. von Dobschütz, *Die Thessalonicher-Briefe,* MeyerK 7, 9th ed (Göttingen: Vandenhoeck & Ruprecht, 1909), p. 97; K. Lake and H. J. Cadbury, *The Beginnings of Christianity,* 5 vols. (London: Macmillan, 1933), 4:223; B. Rigaux, *Les Epitres aux Thessaloniciens,* EBib (Paris: Gabalda, 1956), p. 424; J. Dupont, *Le Discours de Milet: Testament Pastoral de Saint Paul (Actes 20: 18-36)* (Paris: Les Editions au Cerf, 1962), pp. 299-300; G. Bornkamm, *Paul* (New York: Harper & Row, 1971), p. 12; Haenchen, *Acts,* p. 534, n. 3; and W. Michaelis, "σκηνοποιός," *TDNT* 7 (1971): 393-94. Cf. further Silva, "Fabricantes de tiendas," pp. 132-33.

15. See W. Bauer, *Griechisch-deutsches Wörterbuch zu den Schriften des Neuen Testaments,* 5th ed. (Berlin: Töpelmann, 1958), p. 1496. (This entry is significantly longer than that of the 4th edition, which is the basis of BAG.) Why Bauer thinks that tents would not have been made in cities is puzzling. For a tentmaker in Athens, see Aelian *V. H.* 2.1 (p. 16, 7, Dilts).

16. See H. Blümner, *Technologie und Terminologie der Gewerbe und Künste bei Griechen und Römern,* 4 vols., 2d ed. of vol. 1 only (Leipzig and Berlin: Teubner, 1912), 1:273, and T. R. S. Broughton, "Roman Asia,"*An Economic Survey of Ancient Rome,* 6 vols., ed. T. Frank (Baltimore: John Hopkins, 1938), 5:499-916, esp. 823-24.

17. See, e.g., ps.-Socrates *ep.* 13.1 (p. 250, 28, Malherbe), which depicts Simon the shoemaker as also capable of making leather thongs and other leather products. For the many products made from leather, see Blümner, *Technologie, 1:273.* On the specialized names of trades, see A. Burford, *Craftsmen in Greek and Roman Society* (London: Thames & Hudson, 1972), pp. 96-101.

18. For details, see pp. 24-25.

19. *T. Qidd.* 1.11. For this view, see Lightfoot, *Notes,* p. 27; A. T. Geoghegan, *The Attitude towards Labor in Early Christianity and Ancient Culture* (Washington, D.C.: Catholic University of America, 1945), p. 108; and Burchard, *Der dreizehnte Zeuge,* p. 39, n. 58.

20. *M. 'Abot* 2.2.

21. Bornkamm, *Paul,* p. 12.

22. Bruce, *Paul,* p. 108. Others include C. von Weizsäcker, *The Apostolic Age of the Christian Church,* 2 vols. (London: Williams & Norgate, 1897), 1:301; Zahn, *Apostelgeschichte,* pp. 633-34; Jeremias, "Zöllner," p. 299; Michaelis, "Σκηνοποιός," p. 394; and Silva, "Fabricantes de tiendas," p. 134.

23. On the issue of Paul and Gamaliel, see the balanced discussion in Lake and Cadbury, *Beginnings,* 4: 278-79. For the view that Paul was not a student of Gamaliel, see M. Enslin, "Paul and Gamaliel," *JR* 7 (1927): 360-75, and Haenchen, *Acts,* p. 625.

24. See S. Safrai, "Education and the Study of the Torah," *The Jewish People in the First Century,* 2 vols. to date, eds. S. Safrai and M. Stern (Philadelphia: Fortress, 1976), 2:945-70, esp. 958.

25. So Burchard, *Der dreizehnte Zeuge,* pp. 32-33.

26. See, e.g., E. E. Urbach, "Class-Status and Leadership in the World of the Palestinian Sages," *Proceedings of the Israel Academy of Sciences and Humanities,* 2 vols. (Jerusalem: Central, 1968), 2:38-74, esp. 68: "The question of the livelihood and maintenance of scholars was decisive. . . . Poverty and need were the portion of the leading scholars in the Usha period. This situation resulted in many combining their Torah-study with work or a craft."

27. See *b. Ber.* 28a and *b. Pesah.* 34a.

28. See *b. Ta'an* 23a-b; *b. Yoma* 35b; and *b. Sabb.* 31a. According to S. Kalischer ("Die Wertschätzung der Arbeit in Bibel und Talmud," *Judaica: Festschrift zu H. Cohens siebzigstem Geburtstag* [Berlin: Cassirer, 1912], pp. 580-98), the Talmud names over one hundred rabbis who worked, but the overwhelming majority of them belonged to the Usha period or later, as is clear from a perusal of the exhaustive lists in S. Meyer, *Arbeit und Handwerk im Talmud* (Berlin: Benzian, 1878), pp. 23-36.

29. So Urbach, "Palestinian Sages," p. 61.

30. On the form-critical analysis of these traditions, see J. Neusner, *The Rabbinic Traditions about the Pharisees before 70,* 3 vols. (Leiden: Brill, 1971), 1:182 (Abba Hilkiah) and p. 259 (Hillel). Safrai ("Education," pp. 964-65) speaks of first century Pharisaic teachers and students being supported in other ways: teachers by gifts or, if they were priests, by tithes, and students by familial support. In other words, it is difficult to see pre-70 Pharisees anticipating in any normative sense the later rabbinic self-understanding regarding work. Thus, if Paul worked as a Pharisaic student, his working probably had as little to do with his Pharisaic self-understanding as Cleanthes' working while a student of Zeno (see Diogenes Laertius, 7.168-70) had with Stoic self-understanding.

31. See Safrai, "Education," p. 958.

32. Plato *Protag.* 328A. For the early empire: Dio *Orat.* 4.47; 7.111; 71.4; and Lucian *Abd.* 22.

33. See Dio *Orat.* 55.2.

34. The Oxyrhynchus papyri allow us to document a family of weavers through four generations. See P. Oxy. 2.288 (A.D. 22–25) (Tryphon's grandfather, father, and two uncles); P. Oxy. 2.322 desc. (A.D. 36) (Tryphon's brother); P. Oxy. 1.39 (A.D. 52) (Tryphon himself); P. Oxy. 2.310 desc. (A.D. 56) and 2.275 (A.D. 66) (Tryphon's sons). On Tryphon, see E. Brewster, "A Weaver of Oxyrhynchus," *TAPA* 58 (1927): 132–54; Brewster, "In Roman Egypt," *CW* 29 (1935): 25–29; and M. Biscottini, "L' Archivio di Tryphon tesstitore di Oxyrhynchos," *Aegyptus* 46 (1966): 60–90 and 186–292. For more examples of family trades, see P. Oxy. 7. 1029 (A.D. 107); 36.2773 (A.D. 82); Lucian *Somn.* 7; and Burford, *Craftsmen*, pp. 82–87.

35. Lucian, e.g., was apprenticed, briefly at any rate, to his uncle (so Lucian *Somn.* 2–3), and Tryphon, presumably because of failing eyesight (see P. Oxy. 1.39 [A.D. 52]), had to apprentice his son Thoönis to a local weaver (so P. Oxy. 2.275 [A.D. 66]; cf. Brewster, "Roman Egypt," p. 29).

36. On apprentice contracts, see esp. W. L. Westermann, "Apprentice Contracts and the Apprentice System in Roman Egypt," *CPh* 9 (1914): 295–315; A. Zambon, "Διδασκαλικαί," *Aegyptus* 15 (1935): 3–66; and J. Herrmann, "Vertragsinhalt und Rechtsnatur der διδασκαλικαί," *JJP* 11–12 (1957–58): 119–39. On the parallels between Egyptian practice and that in Syria, as known from Lucian's *Somnium,* see Westermann, "Apprentice Contracts," p. 312.

37. See esp. the discussions in Westermann, "Apprentice Contracts," pp. 312–14, and Zambon, "Διδασκαλικαί," p. 33. For Jewish practice, cf. Safrai, "Education," p. 952: " . . . a man was obliged to provide for instruction for his son until the age of twelve and then to begin to teach him a craft and slowly to introduce him to work." For the range of ages, note, e.g., that Lucian was probably fourteen when apprenticed to his uncle (cf. Lucian *Somn.* 16, and Westermann, "Apprentice Contracts," p. 312), whereas a certain boy, not yet twelve, was already promising as a silver-engraver (cf. Burford, *Craftsmen,* p. 182).

38. These apprentice contracts stipulate that the apprentice is to be in the workshop "daily from sunrise to sunset" (see, e.g., P. Oxy. 4.725, 11–12 [A.D. 183]; 14.1647, 19–21 [late second century A.D.]; and Herrmann, "Vertragsinhalt," p. 122). They also stipulate that the apprentice is allowed so many days off per year, sometimes twenty days (see, e.g., P. Oxy. 4.725, 35–37 [A.D. 183]) or at least as often as the teacher took a holiday (cf. Herrmann, "Vertragsinhalt," p. 121). Lucian's comment, that artisans worked all but one or two days per month (*Par.* 15), would thus be about right. In Paul's case, however, the weekly Sabbath rest would have greatly increased the number of holidays, explaining, incidentally, why

Jews would thus have been regarded as lazy (so, e.g., Juvenal *Sat.* 14.105-6).

39. See Bruce, *Paul,* p. 37, citing the suggestion of Sir William Calder. On the military use of tents, see G. Webster, *The Roman Imperial Army of the First and Second Centuries A.D.* (New York: Funk & Wagnalls, 1969), pp. 167-68.

40. The probable length of Paul's apprenticeship is difficult to determine, since the apprentice contracts contain none concerning leatherworking of any kind. The suggestion of two or three years is simply an average, based on all the papyri listed in Zambon, "Διδασκαλικαί," pp. 14-15. Cf. further Westermann, "Apprentice Contracts," p. 309, and Burford, *Craftsmen,* p. 90.

41. The discipline and standards are evident in the specific incidents involving, on the one hand, one of Cerdon's slaves, who was harshly disciplined for sleeping at his workbench (so Herondas, 7.6-9 [p. 47, Cunningham]), and, on the other hand, Lucian, whose mistake with a chisel prompted a beating from his teacher (so Lucian *Somn.* 3-4). Note also the general stipulations of teachers that apprentices "do everything they were ordered to do" (see, e.g., P. Oxy. 41.2971, 9-12 [A.D. 66]), and that they be neither "idle nor disobedient" (see, e.g., P. Oxy. 4.725, 40 [A.D. 183]). Cf. further Herrmann, "Vertragsinhalt," p. 130, and Burford, *Craftsmen,* pp. 91-92.

42. Note especially the clause obligating the teacher to make the apprentice "a perfect worker in the said craft, just as able as the master himself" (so P. Oxy. 31.2586, 45-48 [A.D. 253]; cf. P. Oxy. 2.322, 19-20 [A.D. 36] [text now available in M. Biscottini, "Archivio," pp. 210-11]). Cf. further Zambon, "Διδασκαλικαί," p. 50.

43. On the high technical proficiency of craftsmen, see Xenophon *Oec.* 15.10; Epictetus *Diss.* 4.6.28; 12.14; Dio *Orat.* 71.2-8; Lucian *Somn.* 9; Diogenes Laertius, 6.70; and Burford, *Craftsmen,* pp. 14-16, 68-69, and passim.

44. On leatherworking, see further Blümner, *Technologie,* 1:278-92, and Lau, *Schuster,* pp. 82-108.

45. Cf. further Blümner, *Technologie,* 1:274-80.

46. So ibid., 1:279.

47. On tentmaking, see further J. McIntyre and I. A. Richmond, "Tents of the Roman Army and Leather from Birdoswald," *TCWA* 34 (1934): 62-90.

48. See ibid., pp. 76-77.

49. See ibid., pp. 77-78.

50. On apprentices receiving tools on completion of their training, see, e.g., P. Oxy. 38.2875, 33-34 (early third century A.D.).

CHAPTER 3

1. Since 1 Corinthians was written at Ephesus (1 Cor. 16:8), the phrase "up to this very moment" (ἄχρι τῆς ἄρτι ὥρας) in 4:12 means that Paul was working at Ephesus at the time.

2. That Paul worked even when in Rome is argued by H. J. Cadbury, "Lexical Notes on Luke-Acts III: Luke's Interest in Lodging, " *JBL* 45 (1926): 305–22, esp. 321–22. Cadbury renders the obscure phrase ἐν τῷ μισθώματι in Acts 28:30 as "on his own earnings." The phrase "may refer . . . to what was paid to Paul as wages for his work rather than to what was paid by Paul for food and lodging" (p. 322). Cadbury's interpretation has been accepted by F. F. Bruce, *The Acts of the Apostles: The Greek Text with Introduction and Commentary* (Grand Rapids: Eerdmans, 1951), p. 480, but rejected in favor of "in his own rented quarters" by H. Conzelmann, *Die Apostelgeschichte*, HNT 7, 2d ed. (Tübingen: Mohr, 1963), p. 96, and by E. Haenchen, *The Acts of the Apostles: A Commentary* (Philadelphia: Westminster, 1971), p. 726, n. 2. Cadbury's thesis has been argued afresh and persuasively by E. Hansack, "Er lebte . . . von seinem eigenen Einkommen (Apg. 28:30)," *BZ* 19 (1975): 249–53. The objections of F. Saum (*BZ* 20 [1976]: 226–29) are answered bv Hansack in "Nochmals zu Apostelgeschichte 28:30," *BZ* 21 (1977): 118–21.

3. This is not to deny that Paul at times received financial help from Christian friends, on which see p. 50.

4. This is especially to be assumed where Paul is said to have stayed for a considerable period of time, as, e.g., at Damascus (Acts 9:19, 23), Pisidian Antioch (13:49), Iconium (14:3), Philippi (16:2), and Athens (17:17). That we are to assume that Paul was working during these stays, even though Luke is silent about the matter, is argued by Haenchen, *Acts,* pp. 511–12.

5. For the variety of travelers, see W. Ramsay, "Roads and Travel (in the NT)," *HDB* 5 (1904): 375–402, to which add runaway slaves (so Epictetus *Diss.* 3.26.1–2), athletes (Epictetus *Diss.* 4.4.30, and Dio *Orat.* 29.6), and prisoners (Ignatius *Eph.* 1:2). On travel, see also A. Deissmann, *Paul: A Study in Social and Religious History,* 2d ed. (London: Hodder & Stoughton, 1926), pp. 35–40, 62–68, 88–89, 213–14, 233–37; and L. Casson, *Travel in the Ancient World* (Toronto: Hakkert, 1974), pp. 115–225.

6. See Casson, *Travel,* pp. 122, 149, 165.

7. See W. Ramsay, *St. Paul the Traveller and Roman Citizen* (New York: Putnam's Sons, 1904), pp. 94–97.

8. On students traveling to a resident philosopher, see, e.g., Epictetus *Diss.* 1.4.23; 17.16; 2.21.12; 3.16.11; 21.8; 23.32; Lucian *Abd.* 4; *Herm.* 23; *Tox.* 27; and P. Oxy. 18.2190 (late first century A.D.).

9. The travels of Apollonius—all around the Greek East to India, to the headwaters of the Nile, and to Rome—are recounted in Philostratus's *Vita Apollonii*. Dio traveled all his life, though his wanderings as an exile and philosopher are especially pertinent (see Dio *Orat.* 1.50-52; 13.10; cf. Philostratus *V. Soph.* 488).

10. See Lucian *Peregr.* 9-19. Note also Lucian *Pseudol.* 10, where a Sophist is described as having traveled in Palestine, Egypt, Phoenicia, Syria, Greece, Italy, and Asia Minor. Philostratus's Sophists also traveled (see, e.g., *V. Soph.* 571, 582).

11. See A. Burford, *Craftsmen in Greek and Roman Society* (London: Thames & Hudson, 1972), pp. 15, 61-67, 79-80, 109, 180. Cf. also R. MacMullen, *Roman Social Relations 50 B.C. to A.D. 284* (New Haven: Yale, 1974), p. 97. Still, the movement of artisans may not have been quite so extensive as these authors suggest. See, e.g., Lucian's recitation of the values of becoming a sculptor, one of which is that an artisan would not have to leave family and homeland (so Lucian *Somn.* 7)—as was the case with Tryphon the weaver of Oxyrhynchus. Cf. also the review of Burford's book by J. Packer in *T & C* 17 (1976): 537-41, esp. 538-40.

12. See esp. P. Mich. 1.52 (251 B.C.) where a potter, having shops in Herakleopolis and Philadelphia, shifted ten workers from one shop to the other. Cf. also P. Oxy. 3.527 (second or early third century A.D.) about a fuller and 34.2727 (third or fourth century A.D.) about a shoemaker and a goldsmith.

13. See, e.g., Seneca *De cons. Helv.* 6.2; *Did.* 12.2-3; Dio *Orat.* 36.25; P. Oxy. 2.252 (A.D. 19) about a weaver; 17. 2153 (third century A.D.) about a carpenter and a builder; and 33.2669 (A.D. 41-54) about a bronze-smith.

14. See, e.g., Lucian *Hist. conscr.* 16.

15. On sea travel by means of finding some ship that was heading in the same direction, see Epictetus *Diss.* 3.9.14; Dio *Orat.* 7.2-7; Achilles Tatius, 2.31.5-6; ps.-Lucian *Asin.* 55; and Casson, *Travel,* 152-58. On Paul's various sea voyages, see the brief comments of Haenchen, *Acts,* pp. 702-3.

16. Summer was the time to travel (so Dio *Orat.* 36.1); winter travel was discouraged and dangerous (so ps.-Chion *ep.* 12 [p. 62, 21-22, Düring]; Chariton, 3.5.1 [p. 57, 27-28, Hercher]; and Lucian *Demon.* 35). Cf. further Ramsay, "Roads and Travel," pp. 376-77.

17. That the hunger and thirst and cold were due to the hardships of travel (cf. also 1 Cor. 4:11 and 2 Cor. 6:5) is argued by J. Weiss, *Der erste Korintherbrief,* MeyerK 5, 9th ed. (Göttingen: Vandenhoeck & Ruprecht, 1910), p. 111. See also Dio *Orat.* 7.55, and Lucian *Merc. cond.* 2.

18. See, e.g., Seneca *epp.* 57.1-2 and 96.3.

19. On dangers from brigands, see, e.g., Seneca *De ben.* 4.17.4; Luke 10:30; Dio *Orat.* 46.2; Lucian *Alex.* 44; Achilles Tatius, 3.9; and ps.-Lu-

cian *Asin.* 22. On dangers of shipwreck, see, e.g., Seneca *ep.* 45.2; *De otio* 8.4; Epictetus *Diss.* 2.6.20; 16.22-23; 3.9.3; Dio *Orat.* 77/78.7; and Achilles Tatius, 3.1-5.

20. Like Paul, Apollonius had certain constant travel companions, such as Damis, but on one occasion his travel party totaled thirty-four (so Philostratus *V. Apoll.* 4.37).

21. See, e.g., Epictetus *Diss.* 4.1.91.

22. See Dio *Orat.* 36.7-17.

23. See Aulus Gellius *N. A.* 12.5. For other travel conversations, see Dio *Orat.* 10.1; ps.-Diogenes *ep.* 2 (p. 92, Malherbe); and Aulus Gellius *N. A.* 16.6.1.

24. See Philostratus *V. Soph.* 618 (oratory); Seneca, *epp.* 48.1; 72.2 (letterwriting); and Philostratus *V. Soph.* 488 (reading). Note also a Stoic traveler who had the fifth (now lost) book of Epictetus's *Dissertationes* in his baggage (so Aulus Gellius *N. A.* 19.1.14). Note also that Gellius, during a stopover on his way home, purchased several books and read them the next two nights while waiting for his boat to sail (so *N. A.* 9.4.1-5).

25. See, e.g., Aulus Gellius *N. A.* 2.21.1-2; Philostratus *V. Apoll.* 6.19; and Casson, *Travel,* p. 156.

26. See, e.g., Epictetus *Diss.* 2.19.15-16 (on shipwreck), and Philostratus *V. Apoll.* 4.15 (on shipbuilding and navigating).

27. On lodging at an inn, see, e.g., Seneca *De ben.* 6.15; Luke 10:34-35; Achilles Tatius, 5.2.3; 7.6.6; Philostratus *V. Apoll.* 4.39; and Casson, *Travel,* pp. 200-211.

28. Hospitality was extended to Paul also by Judas (Acts 9:11 and 17), by the Jerusalem church (15:3-4; 21:17), by the Philippian jailer (16:33-34), by several churches as he was en route to Jerusalem (21:4, 7, 8, 16), and later by the church in Puteoli (28:14). Paul looked forward to the hospitality of Christian hosts in Corinth, Colossae, and Rome (so 1 Cor. 16:6; Philem. 22; and Rom. 15:23-24). On hospitality, see also A. J. Malherbe, "The Inhospitality of Diotrephes," *God's Christ and His People: Studies in honour of N. A. Dahl,* ed. J. Jervell and W. Meeks (Oslo: Universitetsforlaget, 1977), pp. 222-32, esp. pp. 223-26. For travelers staying with friends, or with friends of friends, see, e.g., 3 John 5-8; Parthenius, 18.1; and ps.-Lucian *Asin.* 1-2. The hospitality extended to Paul, due to shipwreck, by strangers on Malta (cf. Acts 28:7-10) was also not unusual (see Seneca *De ben.* 4.11.3; 37.1; Dio *Orat.* 7.2-20, 55-58; and Achilles Tatius, 6.9.3).

29. On bath, board, and bed, see ps.-Lucian *Asin.* 7, and Casson, *Travel,* pp. 209-18. On providing travel supplies—the technical term is προπέμπειν—see Malherbe, "Inhospitality," p. 223.

30. On the length of one's stay with a host, see, e.g., *Did.* 11.5; ps.-Lucian *Am.* 8-9; *Asin.* 3; Philostratus *V. Apoll.* 2.23, 5.10.

31. Acts is usually explicit: one day (21:7), three days (9:9; 28:7), and seven days (20:6; 21:4; 28:14).

32. So Haenchen, *Acts,* p. 495, n. 3. Incidentally, inns, for all their bad press (see Malherbe, "Inhospitality," p. 223), could be good (so Epictetus *Diss.* 2.23.36).

33. See C. A. Forbes, "Expanded Uses of the Greek Gymnasium," *CPh* 40 (1945): 32-42, esp. 35.

34. Apollonius frequently stayed in temples (so Philostratus *V. Apoll.* 4.40; 5.20; 8.15). Note also that Diogenes is depicted as staying in a temple in Rhodes until finding a host (see ps.-Diogenes *ep.* 37.1-2 [p. 154, Malherbe]). Cf. also Achilles Tatius, 8.7.2.

35. See S. Safrai, "The Synagogue," *The Jewish People in the First Century,* 2 vols. to date, ed. S. Safrai and M. Stern (Philadelphia: Fortress, 1976), 2:908-44, esp. 943.

36. Note, e.g., that Clitophon is depicted as staying in an Alexandrian inn for at least six months (so Achilles Tatius, 5.8.2.).

37. Luke's mention of three Sabbaths (Acts 17:2) should not be taken to mean that after only three weeks in Thessalonica Paul left for Beroea (17:10-15). Rather, a period of several months is to be presumed, in part to allow for the several gifts to be sent to Paul from Philippi (so Phil. 4:16, on which see Conzelmann, *Apostelgeschichte,* p. 95, and E. Best, *A Commentary on the First and Second Epistles to the Thessalonians,* HNTC [New York: Harper & Row, 1972], pp. 5, 104).

38. It is sometimes argued that Paul's use of Titius Justus's house for missionary work (cf. Acts 18:7) also entailed a change of residence, that is, a move from the house of Aquila and Priscilla (so, e.g., Haenchen, *Acts,* p. 539; and G. Theissen, "Soziale Schichtung in der korinthischen Gemeinde," *ZNW* 65 [1974]: 232-72, esp. 253). But this view underestimates the missionary possibilities of Aquila's workshop and overestimates Paul's financial independence as a result of the provisions sent from Macedonia (cf. 2 Cor. 11:8-9), on which see p. 50.

39. In Ephesus, e.g., Paul is likely to have lodged for at least part of his three-year sojourn (cf. Acts 20:31) in the household of Aquila and Priscilla (cf. 18:19; 19:1; and Deissmann, *Paul,* p. 237).

40. See B. Frier, "The Rental Market in Early Imperial Rome, " *JRS* 67 (1977): 27-37, esp. 30-34.

41. See pp. 55-56.

42. See Lucian *Merc. cond.* 3.

43. See ibid., 20 and 37.

44. Lucian's and Paul's use of βάρος (and its various compounds) is technical. Other examples include: Dio *Orat.* 40.7; Philostratus *V. Soph.* 600; P. Oxy. 3.487, 10-11 (A.D. 156); 8.1159, 2-3 (late third century A.D.); 12.1481, 13 (early second century A.D.); and P. Mich. inv. 347, 21 (third

century A.D.), the last example being published by H. C. Youtie ("The Stubborn Potter," *ZPE* 24 [1977]: 129–32).

45. On these gifts, see p. 50.

46. It is difficult to determine whether Priscilla was also understood by Luke's tradition to have been a tentmaker alongside her husband, but I think not (so also W. Michaelis, "Σκηνοποιός," *TDNT* 7 [1971]: 393–94, esp. 393). Had tents been a product of weavers, the likelihood would be better, since weaving was often, though not exclusively, a woman's trade (so Xenophon *Oec.* 7.5, 41; 10.10; Musonius *frag.* 4 [p. 46, 13–27, Lutz]; Juvenal *Sat.* 11.69; Lucian *D. Meretr.* 6.293; and Diogenes Laertius, 6.98).

47. For a parallel to Luke's language, see Dio *Orat.* 7.2: some fishermen, on being shipwrecked on Euboea, decide to stay (μένειν) and work with (συνερλάζεσθαι) some purple-fishers on the island.

48. See, e.g., T. Zahn, *Die Apostelgeschichte des Lukas*, KNT 5, 2d ed. (Leipzig and Erlangen: Deichert, 1921), p. 634; K. Lake and H. J. Cadbury, *The Beginnings of Christianity*, 5 vols. (London: Macmillan, 1933), 4:205; and Haenchen, *Acts*, p. 512.

49. See Frier, "Rental Market," pp. 27–30.

50. We can appreciate Paul's self-sufficiency when we note how dependent on their families were the students who had left home and had traveled to another city in order to study with a philosopher; they regularly received provisions, mostly foodstuffs, from home and even had a family slave along to help support them (see, e.g., Epictetus *Diss.* 2.21.12–14; ps.-Chion *ep.* 6 [pp. 54 and 56, Düring]; and esp. P. Oxy. 18.2190, 37–64 [late first century A.D.]). It was clearly difficult to live away from home and from one's source of income and support.

51. On the imperfect, see Conzelmann, *Apostelgeschichte*, p. 105.

52. Cf. 2 Cor. 6:5; 11:27; and H. Windisch, *Der zweite Korintherbrief*, MeyerK 6, 9th ed. (Göttingen: Vandenhoeck & Ruprecht, 1924), pp. 205, 359.

53. So J. Frame, *A Critical and Exegetical Commentary on the Epistles of St. Paul to the Thessalonians*, ICC (Edinburgh: Clark, 1912), p. 102.

54. So also Ramsay, *St. Paul*, p. 271, and A. T. Geoghegan, *The Attitude towards Labor in Early Christianity and Ancient Culture* (Washington, D.C.: Catholic University of America, 1945), pp. 109–10.

55. See, e.g., P. Oxy. 4.725, 12 (A.D. 183). The phrase is conventional: P. Oxy. 14.1647, 20–21 (late second century A.D.); 31. 2586, 13–14 (A. D. 253); and 41.2977, 36–37 (A. D. 239). Cf. further J. Herrmann, "Vertragsinhalt und Rechtsnatur der διδασκαλικαί," *JJP* 11–12 (1957–58): 119–39, esp. 122. On working during the day, see P. Oxy. 18.2190, 49–51 (late first century A.D.); P. Mich. 8.465, 14–15 (A.D. 107); 466, 21–22 (A. D. 107); Lucian *Fug.* 17 and *Tox.* 31.

56. See Lucian *Gall.* 1. Cf. also Cerdon's complaint of being in his shop night and day (so Herondas, 7.40 [p. 48, Cunningham]).

57. See B. Metzger, *A Textual Commentary on the Greek New Testament* (London: United Bible Societies, 1971), p. 470.

58. So, e.g., Conzelmann, *Apostelgeschichte*, p. 111 (on the Western text). On the whole verse, see Ramsay, *St. Paul*, pp. 270-71; Lake and Cadbury, *Beginnings*, 4:239; and Haenchen, *Acts*, p. 559, 561. On leaving work early, see also Seneca, *De tranqu. animi* 17.7 (4 P.M. or even noon), and Lucian, *Tox.* 31 (noon). Paul's lecturing in the afternoon would not have been typical, as teachers usually used the morning hours (see, e.g., Epictetus *Diss.* 1.10.8; Lucian *Nigr.* 2 and *Timon* 54). Still, Paul would not have been alone; Seneca's teacher Metronax lectured at 2 P.M. (so Seneca *ep.* 76.1).

59. On workshops, see Burford, *Craftsmen*, pp. 78-82, and L. Casson, "The Athenian Upper Class and New Comedy," *TAPA* 106 (1976): 29-59, esp. 35-41.

60. Simon's shop was in his house (see D. B. Thompson, "The House of Simon the Shoemaker," *Archaeology* 13 [1960]: 234-40). Cerdon is also depicted as having his shoemaking shop in his house (so Herondas, 6.63 [p. 46, Cunningham]). See also Demosthenes *Orat.* 27.24-25; 48.12; P. Tebt. 1.38 (113 B.C.); and PGM 12.104.

61. See J. Packer, "Housing and Population in Imperial Ostia and Rome," *JRS* 57 (1967): 80-95, esp. 80-81, 83, 85.

62. See, e.g., Dio *Orat.* 40.8-9; and Casson, "Athenian Upper Class," pp. 35-36.

63. Burford, *Craftsmen*, pp. 80-82.

64. So, e.g., Simon's workshop, which was located just outside the southwest corner of the Athenian *agora* (cf. Thompson, "House," p. 235). See Lysias *Orat.* 24.19-20; Chariton, 1.12.5 (p. 21, 13-14, Hercher); and Dio *Orat.* 46.9.

65. See Plutarch *De gen. Socr.* 580E. The shoemaker Micyllus had a neighbor of the same trade (so Lucian *Gall.* 14). See also Dio *Orat.* 40.9; Lucian *Pisc.* 13; and the excellent discussion in MacMullen, *Roman Social Relations*, pp. 71-73.

66. So, e.g., Simon the shoemaker (cf. Thompson, "House," p. 240). So also Tryphon the weaver with his two sons (cf. E. H. Brewster, "In Roman Egypt," *CW* 29 [1935]: 25-29, esp. 28-29). Other examples are P. Oxy. 3.527 (second or early third century A.D.) about two fullers and P. Mich. inv. 347 (third century A.D.) about one potter.

67. See, e.g., Lysias *Orat.* 12.8-19. In addition, see the large shops cited by Casson, "Athenian Upper Class," p. 36, to which add: P. Mich. 1.52 (251 B.C.); P. Oxy. 22.2340 (A.D. 192); and Dio *Orat.* 7.104.

68. So Burford, *Craftsmen*, p. 79.

69. See Herondas, 7.44 (p. 48, Cunningham). Another shoemaker's shop had ten (so Aeschines, 1.97).

70. See, e.g., Seneca *ep.* 56.4 (noisy workshop); Lucian *Somn.* 6 (sculptor covered with marble dust); Juvenal *Sat.* 10.130–32; and Lucian *Sacr.* 6 (smiths working in smoky shops and covered with ashes). Cf. further Burford, *Craftsmen,* p. 72.

71. On weavers' equipment, see, e.g., P. Oxy. 7.1035 (A.D. 143) and 36.2773 (A.D. 82). Note that Tryphon was not able to purchase his own loom until he was forty-three years old (so P. Oxy. 2.264 [A.D. 54]); presumably, he had rented one until this time.

72. See Teles *frag.* IV[B] (p. 48, 21–31, O'Neil).

73. See Herondas, 7.6 (p. 47, Cunningham).

74. For pictures of tables and stools, see H. Blümner, *Technologie und Terminologie der Gewerbe und Künste bei Griechen und Römern,* 4 vols., 2d ed. of vol. 1 only (Leipzig and Berlin: Teubner, 1912), 1:285, 287. Cf. O. Lau, "Schuster und Schusterhandwerk in der griechisch-römischen Literatur und Kunst" (diss., Bonn, 1967), pp. 71–75.

75. For details, see Blümner, *Technologie,* 1:278–84, and Lau, *Schuster,* pp. 76–81.

76. See Herondas, 7.5, 14, 19, 53 (pp. 47–49, Cunningham), and Blümner, *Technologie,* 1:289.

77. See, e.g., Cerdon's sales pitch to the ladies brought to his shop by his patroness Metro (so Herondas, 7.14–35 and 49–63 [pp. 48–49, Cunningham]). For apprentices, see Blümner, *Technologie,* 1:286.

78. See, e.g., Diogenes Laertius, 2.122.

79. So Chariton, 1.12.5 (p. 21, 13–14, Hercher).

80. See, e.g., Seneca *De ira* 3.22.2; Chariton, 7.2.5 (p. 125, 15, Hercher); Dio *Orat.* 12.18; Achilles Tatius, 3.23.4; and G. Webster, *The Roman Imperial Army of the First and Second Centuries A.D.* (New York: Funk & Wagnalls, 1969), pp. 167–68. Cf. also J. McIntyre and I. A. Richmond, "Tents of the Roman Army and Leather from Birdoswald," *TCWA* 34 (1934): 62–90.

81. See ps.-Lucian *Am.* 8.

82. See Achilles Tatius, 2.33.1. Cf. Chariton, 3.6.2 (p. 59, 22, Hercher).

83. See, e.g., Diodorus Siculus, 14.109.1; Dio *Orat.* 9.22; Lucian *Herod.* 8; ps.-Lucian *Nero* 2–3; Aelian *V. H.* 4.9 (p. 66, 26–27, Dilts); and Casson, *Travel,* pp. 90–91.

84. See, e.g., P. Oxy. 2.251 (A.D. 44), which records one of many people "without a trade" (ἄτεχνος) who fled Oxyrhynchus due to lack of means; *Did.* 12.4, which presumes that Christians without trades require the aid of the church; and Dio *Orat.* 7.11–20, which tells of two herdsmen who, trying to make ends meet, could find no jobs in the city, especially in the winter.

85. See, e.g., the exceedingly grim description of miners in Diodorus Siculus, 3.12.2–13.2.

86. See Dio *Orat.* 7.112, and *Did.* 12.3.

87. This sentiment was shared by the working class, as evidenced in Lucian's father's reasons for apprenticing Lucian to a sculptor (see Lucian *Somn.* 1–2). Cf. also Petronius *Sat.* 46, and Lucian *Merc. cond.* 6.

88. So, e.g., Philenus the smith and Callides the painter (see Lucian *D. Meretr.* 6.293 and 8.30). Cf. Juvenal *Sat.* 14.272–74.

89. After many years at his trade Tryphon was able to purchase his own loom (so P. Oxy. 2.264 [A.D. 54]) and half of a three-story house (so P. Oxy. 1.99 [A.D. 55]). Cerdon's shoes typically supplied his necessities (so Herondas, 7.73 [p. 49, Cunningham]), but the shoes required for an upcoming wedding portended larger profits (so Herondas, 7.83–90 [p. 50, Cunningham]). Note also a prosperous barber in Juvenal *Sat.* 10.225–26. Even luckier was Micyllus's neighbor and fellow tradesman Simon, who became rich due to an inheritance (see Lucian *Gall.* 14).

90. See PGM 4.2437–40. Cf. also PGM 8.61–63 and 12.103–4.

91. See, e.g., P. Oxy. 2.252 (A.D. 19) about a weaver and 33.2669 (A.D. 41–54) about a bronze-smith.

92. See Dio *Orat.* 77/78.3–14.

93. See Lucian *Fug.* 13–14. Cf. also Juvenal *Sat.* 3.293–94; Lucian *Gall.* 22; and Lau, *Schuster,* pp. 40–41.

94. The experiences that caused these hardships are usually identified as having been travel (see above n. 17) or imprisonment (so Windisch, *Zweiter Korintherbrief,* p. 359), but surely his daily experiences as a tentmaker were also a cause (ibid.). Paul's nakedness (2 Cor. 11:27: γυμνότης; cf. 1 Cor. 4:11) requires further explanation. The word is not to be taken literally (i.e., being stark naked) but is to be seen as meaning "being insufficiently dressed" (see, e.g., Epictetus *Diss.* 3.22.45–47, where being "naked" means having only one shabby cloak; cf. G. Heinrici, *Der erste Brief an die Korinther,* MeyerK 5, 7th ed. [Göttingen: Vandenhoeck & Ruprecht, 1888], p. 129, and A. Robertson and A. Plummer, *A Critical and Exegetical Commentary on the First Epistle of Paul to the Corinthians,* ICC, 2d ed. [Edinburgh: Clark, 1914], p. 86). If related to Paul's tentmaking, his "nakedness" would refer either to his general lack of clothing (cf. Lucian *Gall.* 20, and Juvenal *Sat.* 14.300–303) or to his being "stripped" for work (cf. Plato *Resp.* 372A; Diodorus Siculus, 3.13.2; Lucian *Somn.* 6; Diogenes Laertius, 2.131; and Blümner, *Technologie,* 1:286–87).

95. In his *Somnium,* Lucian presents the advantages of becoming a sculptor: pride of carrying on a family tradition, strength from doing manual labor, and reknown for being a master craftsman (*Somn.* 7–8). On

the artisan's place in society, see also Lau, *Schuster,* pp. 16–42, and Mac-Mullen, *Roman Social Relations,* pp. 57–87, 114–20.

96. Herondas, 7.44 (p. 48, Cunningham). Cf. also P. Oxy. 2.262 (A.D. 61) and 41.2957 (A.D. 91). See further M. I. Finley, *The Ancient Economy* (Berkeley: University of California, 1973), pp. 73–74.

97. See Aristotle *Pol.* 1337b 12–13; Lucian *Somn.* 13, *Merc. cond.* 23, and *Timon* 7. Leatherworkers would also have assumed this position (see p. 24).

98. Cicero *De off.* 1.42.150. See also MacMullen, *Roman Social Relations,* p. 115.

99. See esp. Lucian *Somn.* 9 and 13. Cf. also Plutarch *De poet. aud.* 28D, and *De fort. Rom.* 318C. See Xenophon of Ephesus, 5.8.3–4 (pp. 61, 26—62, 5, Papanikolaou), which contains the lament of the aristocratic Habrocomes at being humiliated when forced to take up stonecutting.

100. See, e.g., Xenophon *Oec.* 4.3, and Lucian *Somn.* 10.

101. See, e.g., Xenophon *Oec.* 4.3, and Aristotle *Pol.* 1319b 28.

102. See Lucian *Gall.* 2. Cf. also ps.-Socrates *ep.* 9.4 (p. 246, 29–33, Malherbe), and Epictetus *Diss.* 1.19.16–23.

103. See P. Oxy. 2.264, 17–18 (A.D. 54).

104. See Lucian *Somn.* 8.

105. See Lucian *Vit. auct.* 7 and 11.

106. See Xenophon *Oec.* 4.2; Musonius *frag.* 11 (pp. 80, 29—82, 5, Lutz); and Dio *Orat.* 7.110.

107. See Seneca *epp.* 88.21; 90.15–19; and Dio *Orat.* 7.117. Cf. also Cicero *De off.* 1.42.151; Seneca *ep.* 8.5; *De cons. Helv.* 10.5; Plutarch *De vit. aere al.* 830E; and ps.-Lucian *Am.* 34.

108. See Seneca *epp.* 4.10; 60.2–3; 95.19; *De prov.* 3.6; *De cons. Helv.* 10.2–5; Musonius *frag.* 18B (p. 118, 31–32, Lutz) and 19 (p. 122, 20–22); ps.-Diogenes *ep.* 1 (p. 93, 2–6, Malherbe); ps.-Crates *ep.* 7 (p. 59, 7, Malherbe); and Juvenal *Sat.* 14.267–75.

109. See, e.g., Seneca *De const. sap.* 14.3; Dio *Orat.* 7.114–15; 34.23; and Lucian *Cat.* 15. Cf. also MacMullen, *Roman Social Relations,* pp. 138–41.

110. See, e.g., P. Oxy. 2.284, 285 (A.D. 50) on extortion of two weavers by tax collector.

111. See, e.g., Lucian *Gall.* 9–11.

112. See Lucian *Cat.* 15, and Philostratus *V. Apoll.* 3.23.

113. So Zeno, on whom see H. C. Baldry, "Zeno's Ideal State," *JHS* 79 (1959): 3–25, esp. 10–11.

114. See further my article "Paul's tentmaking and the Problem of His Social Class," *JBL* 97 (1978): 555–64.

115. So rightly Weiss, *Erster Korintherbrief,* p. 112.

116. See Judge, "St. Paul and Classical Society," *JAC* 15 (1972): 19-36, esp. 28, 32.

117. See Xenophon *Mem.* 4.2.22.

118. Ibid., 3.10.1-15; 4.2.1-39; and *Oec.* 6.13. According to Diogenes Laertius, 2.21, conversations of Socrates in workshops were also contained in a book by Demetrius of Byzantium. Workshops were, of course, favorite resorts for discussion (see, e.g., Lysias *Orat.* 24.19-20; Isocrates *Areop.* 15; Demosthenes *Orat.* 25.52; and Chariton, 1.12.5 [p. 21, 13-14, Hercher]).

119. See Xenophon *Mem.* 3.10.1-5, 6-8, 9-15.

120. See ibid., 4.2.1.

121. See Diogenes Laertius, 2.122 (thirty-three subjects).

122. On the ubiquity of Socrates' philosophical discussions, see R. E. Wycherley, "Peripatos: The Athenian Philosophical Scene, Part I," *G & R* 8 (1961): 152-63, esp. 157-61.

123. On these gymnasia, see J. Travlos, *Pictorial Dictionary of Ancient Athens* (New York: Prager, 1971), pp. 42-51, 340-41, 345-47. On the gymnasia as settings for educational and intellectual activity of Sophists and philosophers, see Forbes, "Greek Gymnasium," pp. 33-37; Wycherley, "Peripatos: The Athenian Philosophical Scene, Part II," *G & R* 9 (1962): 2-21, esp. 2-15; and J. P. Lynch, *Aristotle's School: A Study of a Greek Educational Institution* (Berkeley: University of California, 1972), pp. 32-83.

124. See further Wycherley, "Athenian Philosophical Scene, Part II," pp. 16-17, and R. E. Wycherley, "The Painted Stoa," *Phoenix* 7 (1953): 20-35.

125. See further Wycherley, "Athenian Philosophical Scene, Part II," pp. 15-16, and R. E. Wycherley, "The Garden of Epicurus," *Phoenix* 13 (1959): 73-77.

126. See, e.g., Diogenes Laertius, 2.25.

127. See the evidence collected in my article "Simon the Shoemaker as an Ideal Cynic," *GRBS* 17 (1976): 43-46.

128. See Teles *frag.* IV[B] (p. 48, 21-31, O'Neil).

129. See ibid., IV[A] (p. 42, 125-27, O'Neil).

130. See ps.-Socrates *epp.* 9.4 (p. 246, 29-31, Malherbe) and 13.1 (p. 250, 26-27).

131. See Lucian *Cat.* 14-29.

132. See Lucian *Fug.* 12-13, 17, 28, 33; *Bis acc.* 6; and *Icar.* 30-31. Note also that in the *Piscator* the goddess Philosophia is portrayed as frequenting not the doorways of the rich, but the Ceramicus, the potters' quarters (see Lucian *Pisc.* 12-13, 34, 40).

133. See Plutarch *Maxime cum princ. phil. diss.* 776B.

134. On the importance of the gymnasia as a social setting for intellec-

tual activity in the early empire, see Epictetus *Diss.* 3.16.14; 4.1.113; Plutarch *Non posse suav. vivi* 1086D; Dio *Orat.* 13.31; and ps.-Crates *ep.* 20 (p. 70, Malherbe). On the stoa, see Lucian *J. Trag.* 4–5, 16–18, 35–51. On the houses of the rich and powerful, see Dio *Orat.* 77/78.34–36; Lucian *Philops.* 6 and 14; *Pisc.* 11–13; *Vit. auct.* 15; and Philostratus *V. Soph.* 520–21, 600. On the philosophers' own living quarters for teaching, see Seneca *ep.* 76.1–4; Epictetus *Diss.* 4.1.177; Dio *Orat.* 15.1; Plutarch *Consol. ad ux.* 609C; Lucian *Nigr.* 1–7; Aulus Gellius *N. A.* 2.2.1–2 and 12.11.1.

135. See Lucian *Icar.* 30–31. Cf. A. T. Geoghegan, *The Attitude towards Labor in Early Christianity and Ancient Culture* (Washington, D.C.: Catholic University of America, 1945), p. 13: "the group that was most hostile to manual labor was that of the philosophers."

136. See Seneca *ep.* 90.7–31.

137. So, e.g., the Sophist Protagoras, a former porter (cf. Aulus Gellius, *N. A.* 5.3.1–6), and the Cynic Monimus, a former banker (cf. Diogenes Laertius, 6.82). Cf. also the generalizations of Lucian *(Fug.* 12–13 and *Bis acc.* 6).

138. On Cleanthes, see Seneca *ep.* 44.3; Epictetus *Diss.* 3.26.23; Plutarch *De vit. aere al.* 830C–D; and Diogenes Laertius, 7.168–69. Note also the two Platonists Menedemus of Eretria and Asclepiades of Phlius, who worked as millers and as builders (so Athenaeus *Deipnos.* 4.168A–B, and Diogenes Laertius, 2.125 and 131).

139. See ps.-Socrates *epp.* 9.4 (p. 246, 29–31, Malherbe), 11 (p. 248, 18–19), and 13.1 (p. 266, 26–27).

140. See ps.-Socrates *ep.* 13.1 (p. 250, 17–26, Malherbe). Cf. ps.-Socrates *ep.* 18.2 (p. 266, 21–26).

141. See ps-Socrates *ep.* 8 (p. 244, 2–4, Malherbe), and my "Simon the Shoemaker," 49–53.

142. See ps.-Socrates *ep.* 12 (p. 250, 10–11, Malherbe).

143. See ps.-Socrates *epp.* 12 (p. 250, 2–12, Malherbe) and 18.2 (p. 266, 21–26).

144. See esp. ps.-Socrates *ep.* 9 (pp. 244–46, Malherbe).

145. See ps.-Socrates *ep.* 13.2 (pp. 250, 31—252, 9, Malherbe). Simon is also ridiculed in *epp.* 9.4 (p. 246, 29–31) and 11 (p. 248, 18–19).

146. On Simon as part of a debate between "strict" and "hedonistic" Cynics, see my "Simon the Shoemaker," pp. 48–53. For these two wings of the Cynic "school," see esp. G. A. Gerhard, "Zur Legende vom Kyniker Diogenes," *ARW* 15 (1912): 388–408.

147. On the necessities of life being easily procured, see, e.g., Teles *frag.* II (p. 8, 30–44, O'Neil); ps.-Diogenes *ep.* 33.3 (p. 140, 30–32, Malherbe); and Diogenes Laertius, 6.22, 58, 104. Cf. also Lucian *Merc. cond.* 24.

148. On begging, see pp. 55–56.

149. See Lucian *Bis acc.* 6, and *Fug.* 28 and 33.

150. On Cynic critiques of the trades, see ps.-Anacharsis, *ep.* 9 (p. 49, 14–25, Malherbe), and ps.-Lucian *Cyn.* 5. Flutists are despised by Antisthenes in Plutarch *Per.* 1.6; perfumers by Diogenes in Teles *frag.* II (p. 12, 104–9, O'Neil); and chefs by Crates in Diogenes Laertius, 6.86.

151. See ps.-Socrates *ep.* 13.1–2 (p. 250, 27–30, Malherbe).

152. Stobaeus *Floril.* 3.5.52 (p. 273, Hense). Cf. a similar aloofness on the part of Diogenes in Lucian *Hist. conscr.* 3.

153. See Lucian *Tox.* 31.

154. See Philostratus *V. Soph.* 488, and H. von Arnim, *Leben und Werke des Dio von Prusa* (Berlin: Weidmann, 1898), pp. 246-48.

155. See Musonius *frag.* 11 (p. 82, 31–33, Lutz). The Cynicizing elements in Musonius's Stoicism are well-known (see, e.g., D. R. Dudley, *A History of Cynicism from Diogenes to the Sixth Century A.D.* [London: Methuen, 1937], pp. 193–96).

156. See Teles *frag.* IV[B] (p. 48, 21–31, O'Neil), and W. G. Rabinowitz, *Aristotle's 'Protrepicus' and the Sources of Its Reconstruction* (Berkeley: University of California, 1957), pp. 28–34, esp. p. 29.

157. For a model study of Paul's use of Cynic traditions, see A. J. Malherbe, "Gentle as a Nurse: The Cynic Background of 1 Thess. 2," *NovT* 12 (1970): 203–17. Cf. also H.-D. Betz, *Der Apostel Paulus und die sokratische Tradition,* BHTh 45 (Tübingen: Mohr, 1972), passim.

158. See, e.g., T. G. Soares, "Paul's Missionary Methods," *Biblical World* 34 (1909): 326–36, esp. 335: Paul's workshop acquaintance with Aquila and Priscilla "may very well suggest *the constant personal evangelism* that Paul must have carried on during his hours of labor with the various fellow-workers with whom he was thrown into companionship" (emphasis added). Haenchen (*Acts,* p. 512) makes a similar claim, but he virtually retracts it elsewhere (see *Acts,* pp. 534, 539). Most scholars assume that Paul could not have carried on his mission from a workshop, as is clear from the exegetical tradition concerning Acts 18:5. The arrival of Silas and Timothy in Corinth, presumably with gifts from Macedonia (see 2 Cor. 11:8-9), is understood as allowing Paul to give up his tentmaking and to preach every day instead of only on the Sabbath (so, e.g., Zahn, *Apostelgeschichte,* p. 649; Lake and Cadbury, *Beginnings,* 4:224; and Conzelmann, *Apostelgeschichte,* p. 105). See also G. Bornkamm, *Paul* (New York: Harper & Row, 1971), p. 69, and F. F. Bruce, *Paul: Apostle of the Heart Set Free* (Grand Rapids: Eerdmans, 1977), p. 252.

159. So, e.g., E. von Dobschütz, *Die Thessalonicher-Briefe,* MeyerK 10, 9th ed. (Göttingen: Vandenhoeck & Ruprecht, 1909), p. 97; and W. Bienert, *Die Arbeit nach der Lehre der Bibel* (Stuttgart: Evangelisches Verlagswerk, 1954), p. 312.

160. Only Frame (*Epistles to the Thessalonians,* p. 4) picks up on Paul's

individual contact with the Thessalonians as going on apart from the synagogue (cf. Acts 17:2), but he does not suggest where these meetings were. Admittedly, Paul's metaphors do not derive from the workshop, as they do, say, in Epictetus (e.g., *Diss.* 2.5.21; 14.4–5; 4.6.28), but Paul did speak of his missionary labors in the same language as his trade (i.e., κόπος); see e.g., 1 Cor. 15:10, Gal. 4:11, and 1 Thess. 3:5.

161. For Stoics and Epicureans in the stoa, see, e.g., Lucian *J. Trag.* 4–5.

162. See S. Safrai, "The Synagogue," 2:908–44, esp. 918.

163. Note again Crates reading in the shop of Philiscus (so Teles *frag.* IV^B [p. 48, 21–22, O'Neil]).

164. Cf. further E. Nestle, "The Aprons and Handkerchiefs of St. Paul," *ExpT* 13 (1901–2): 282, and Conzelmann, *Apostelgeschichte,* p. 111. On the use of a "handkerchief" (σουδάριον) in a magical spell, see PGM 7.826–27 and 36.269–70.

165. For full treatment of these discussions, see G. Agrell, *Work, Toil and Sustenance: An Examination of the View of Work in the New Testament, Taking into Consideration Views Found in Old Testament, Intertestamental and Early Rabbinic Writings* (Lund: Verbum-Håkan Ohlssons, 1976), p. 101–3.

166. For representatives of this view, see C. J. Ellicott, *A Critical and Grammatical Commentary on St. Paul's Epistles to the Thessalonians* (Andover, Mass.: Draper, 1884), pp. 70–71; von Dobschütz, *Thessalonicher-Briefe,* pp. 180–83; Frame, *Epistles to the Thessalonians,* p. 161; B. Rigaux, *Les Epitres aux Thessaloniciens,* EBib (Paris: Gabalda, 1956), pp. 519–21; Best, *Epistles to the Thessalonians,* p. 175; and Agrell, *Work,* p. 103. In contrast, Bienert (*Arbeit,* pp. 370–72) attributes the idleness to the Thessalonians' negative attitude toward work, whereas W. Schmithals (*Paul and the Gnostics* [Nashville: Abingdon, 1972], pp. 114–16) attributes it to an alleged gnostic heresy at Thessalonica.

167. Agrell (*Work,* p. 102) is aware of eschatology having to be imported into the text. See also F. Laub, *Eschatologische Verkündigung und Lebensgestaltung: Eine Untersuchung zum Wirken des Apostels beim Aufbau der Gemeinde in Thessalonike* (Regensburg: Pustet, 1973), pp. 57–58, 174–78.

168. The use of 2 Thess. 3:6–15 to interpret 1 Thess. 4:11–12 is apparent especially in Frame, *Epistles to the Thessalonians,* pp. 160–61.

169. On 1 Thessalonians as a paraenetic letter, see A. J. Malherbe, *Social Aspects of Early Christianity* (Baton Rouge: Louisiana State University, 1977), pp. 22–24.

170. See, e.g., Ellicott, *Epistles to the Thessalonians,* p. 71, and Best, *Epistles to the Thessalonians,* p. 177.

171. M. Dibelius, *An die Thessalonicher I II, an die Philipper,* HNT 11, 3d. ed. (Tübingen: Mohr, 1937), p. 23.

172. The expression is A. D. Nock's (St. Paul [New York: Harper & Row, 1963], p. 154). Those who would agree are legion; see, e.g., von Dobschütz, Thessalonicher-Briefe, p. 180; Best, Epistles to the Thessalonians, p. 176; and Agrell, Work, p. 97.

173. See especially F. Hauck, Die Stellung des Urchristentums zu Arbeit und Geld, BFCT 2, 3 (Gütersloh: Bertelsmann, 1921), pp. 102–3.

174. Cicero De off. 1.42.150.

175. On the representativeness of Cicero's sentiments, see Finley, Ancient Economy, pp. 35–61.

176. See, e.g., Seneca ep. 88.21, and Plutarch Per. 2.1.

177. See Lucian Tox. 18 and 31.

178. See Epictetus Diss. 3.26.6–7, and Plutarch De vit aere al. 830A–B. See also Xenophon of Ephesus 5.8.1–4 (pp. 61, 21—62, 5, Papanikalaou).

179. See Dio Orat. 7.127.

180. On the oration as a whole, see von Arnim, Dio von Prusa, pp. 492–504; on the section treating suitable occupations for the urban poor (7.104–26), see now P. A. Brunt, "Aspects of the Social Thought of Dio Chrysostom and of the Stoics," PCPhS 19 (1973): 9–34, esp. 9–19.

181. See Dio Orat. 3.124–25.

182. See Philostratus V. Soph. 488.

183. See, e.g., Ellicott, Epistles to the Thessalonians, p. 71; Frame, Epistles to the Thessalonians, p. 162; and Agrell, Work, p. 99.

184. For this usage, see also Philodemus Oec. col. 23 (p. 64, 17–19, Jensen); Lucian Salt. 34; P. Oxy, 22.2340, 17–18 (A.D. 192); and Brunt, "Social Thought," pp. 19–26.

185. Recent attempts to emphasize the high social status of some early Christians (so, e.g., H. Kreissig, "Zur sozialen Zusammensetzung der frühchristlichen Gemeinde im ersten Jahrhundert u. Z.," Eirene 6 [1967]: 91–100, and Theissen, "Soziale Schichtung," pp. 231–72) should not obscure the fact that many Christians belonged to the urban poor. See further Malherbe, Social Aspects, pp. 29–59.

186. See Dio Orat. 17.4: more idlers were to be found than men willing to work.

187. See ibid. 17.6–7.

188. See Lucian Somn. 1–2.

189. See, e.g., Frame, Epistles to the Thessalonians, p. 161; Rigaux, Epitres aux Thessaloniciens, p. 521; and Best, Epistles to the Thessalonians, pp. 174–75.

190. Thus rightly von Dobschütz, Thessalonicher-Briefe, p. 180. Cf. also Malherbe, Social Aspects, pp. 24–27.

191. The political connotations of ἡσυχία ("quietism") are particularly evident in the late-first-century epistolary novel, the letters of Chion. See ps.-Chion, epp. 13.3 (p. 64, 21–22, Düring), 14.5 (p. 68, 25), and 16.5–8 (pp. 74, 7—76, 24). On the dating of these letters, see I. Düring, Chion of

Heraclea: A Novel in Letters (Göteborg: Wettergren and Kerbers, 1951), pp. 20-23. Cf. also Plutarch *Quom. adul. ab amico internosc.* 53B; Epictetus *Diss.* 1.10.2; and Dio *Orat.* 34.52.

192. See, e.g., Dio *Orat.* 47.2. Cf. also Plutarch *Praec. ger. reip.* 798E, which describes a career in public life as τὰ κοινὰ πράσσειν, whose opposite is quietism (ἡσυχία) 798F.

193. See Plutarch *De exil.* 602C.

194. See Diogenes Laertius, 10.119 and 143. Epicureans were widely perceived as withdrawn from public life (so, e.g., Seneca *ep.* 90.35; Epictetus *Diss.* 1.23.6; 3.24.39; and Plutarch *Non posse suav. vivi* 1100C).

195. See, e.g., Epictetus *Diss.* 4.8; Dio *Orat.* 34.52; and R. MacMullen, *Enemies of the Roman Order: Treason, Unrest, and Alienation in the Empire* (Cambridge: Harvard, 1966), pp. 50-52.

196. See esp. Musonius *frag.* 11 (pp. 80-84, Lutz), which encourages the philosopher to retire from the city to the country and to support himself at farming. See also Philodemus *Oec.* col. 23 (p. 63, 7-18, Jensen), which also advocates withdrawal to a farm on the part of Epicurean philosophers, who, however, are to let others do the work—in part, to assure the least contact with other men. As a means of livelihood for the philosopher, Musonius deemed his proposal most suitable (πρεπωδέστατος), p. 84, 27, Lutz; Philodemus considered his most seemly (εὐσχημονέστατος), p. 63, 17-18, Jensen. On retirement and working with one's hands, see also Plutarch *Mul. virt.* 257D-E.

197. So, e.g., A. Deissmann, *Light from the Ancient East* (New York: Harper, 1927), pp. 313-14. The maxim in 2 Thess. 3:10—"If someone does not want to work, let him not eat"—may be placed beside such workshop maxims as those repeated by Lucian's uncle: "Well begun is half done" (so Lucian *Somn.* 3), and by Cerdon: "Business requires sales, not just a sales pitch" (so Herondas, 7.49-50, Cunningham).

198. See esp. D. Kienast, "Ein vernachlässigtes Zeugnis für die Reichpolitik Trajans: Die zweite tarsische Rede des Dion von Prusa," *Historia* 20 (1971): 62-80. Kienast argues that the second Tarsian oration (*Orat.* 34) suggests that Dio functioned as a Greek spokesman for Trajan's new policy regarding the administration of the eastern provinces. Dio's advice that the linenworkers of Tarsus be allowed to take part in public life (cf. *Orat.* 34.23) was thus a break with earlier policy, begun under Augustus, that had placed political responsibility in the hands of provincial oligarchies. Accordingly, Paul's advocacy of political quietism for the urban poor would have been consistent with the earlier Augustan policy. Cf. further, G. W. Bowersock, *Augustus and the Greek World* (Oxford: Clarendon, 1965), pp. 85-100 and passim.

199. This point is occasionally made. See Hauck, *Stellung der Urchristentums zu Arbeit,* p. 105, and W. Neil, *The Epistles of Paul to the Thessalonians,* MNTC (London: Hodder & Stoughton, 1950), p. 42.

92 THE SOCIAL CONTEXT OF PAUL'S MINISTRY

200. See, e.g., von Dobschütz, *Thessalonicher-Briefe,* p. 312, and Conzelmann, *Apostelgeschichte,* p. 119.

201. On the paraenetic, rather than apologetic, function of 1 Thess. 2:1-12, see Malherbe, *Social Aspects,* pp. 22-24. Cf. Laub, *Eschatologische Verkündigung,* p. 135.

202. On the role of models in paraenesis, couched in the language of remembrance, see, e.g., Isocrates *Demon.* 9, and Malherbe, *Social Aspects,* p. 24, n. 54.

203. This point would be assured if the γάρ ("for") in 1 Thess. 2:9 confirms the immediately preceding words: "you have become beloved (ἀγαπητοί) to us" (v. 8). But commentators sometimes relate verse 9 to verse 8a (so, e.g., Ellicott, *Epistles to the Thessalonians,* p. 37) or even to verse 7 (so, e.g., Frame, *Epistles to the Thessalonians,* p. 102, and Best, *Epistles to the Thessalonians,* p. 103). In any case, Paul's working as an expression of his love is suggested by the contextual metaphors of nurse (v. 7) and father (v. 11).

204. Musonius *frag.* 11 (p. 82, 26-31, Lutz). For this independence theme, see also 1 Cor. 9:19.

205. See Lucian *Tox.* 31.

206. See Philostratus *V. Soph.* 488, and, for this interpretation, von Arnim, *Dio von Prusa,* p. 247.

207. See Malherbe, "Gentle as a Nurse," p. 217.

208. See, e.g., Lucian *Pisc.* 29-37, 40-42, 47-52; and *Fug.* 30-31.

209. Ps.-Socrates *ep.* 1.1-2 (p. 218, 10-13, Malherbe).

CHAPTER 4

1. See D. L. Dungan, *The Sayings of Jesus in the Churches of Paul: The Use of the Synoptic Tradition in the Regulation of Early Church Life* (Philadelphia: Fortress, 1971), p. 29. According to Dungan, the Philippian church gave Paul "financial support in sufficient amount so that it could be termed a salary. [This church] helped him substantially: several payments at Thessalonica [Phil. 4:15-17], several more at Corinth [2 Cor. 11:8-9], and once while he was in prison [Phil. 2:25-30]." But Paul's language does not imply "salary"—either the word *provisions* (ὀψώνιον) in 2 Cor. 11:8 (cf. C. Caragounis, "Ὀψώνιον: A Reconsideration of Its Meaning," *NovT* 16 [1974]: 35-57, esp. 37-47) or the word *gift* in Phil. 4:17. In addition, the length of time between gifts (see esp. Phil. 4:10) speaks against the interpretation of these gifts being regular enough even to function as a salary. Finally, in 2 Cor. 12:15, where a future trip to Corinth is mentioned, Paul refers only to *his* expense; he could not expect help from Macedonia on that trip.

2. Many scholars interpret Acts 18:5, which reports the arrival of Silas and Timothy from Macedonia, presumably with aid (cf. 2 Cor. 11:8-9), as meaning that Paul then was able to leave his workbench and devote all his time to preaching (cf. Acts 18:5-6). For representatives of this view, see above p. 89, n. 166. This interpretation, however, too readily assumes that Paul could do no missionary work in the workshop, an assumption that needs reconsideration in light of what was said earlier (pp. 37-42). Moreover, the use of a compound verb in 2 Cor. 11:9 (προs-αναπληροῦν) means that the Macedonian aid was only something that filled Paul's needs in addition to his own work. In other words, this aid filled up "what was wanting, after Paul had plied his trade" (so J. B. Lightfoot, *Notes on the Epistles of Paul* [London: Macmillan, 1895], p. 27). Paul continued to work, even when he received occasional support.

3. On the curious notion that Paul was *secretly* receiving financial support from Macedonia, see Dungan, *Churches of Paul,* pp. 4, 12 (n. 1), 22, 28, and 39. Secrecy seems most unlikely. Aquila and Priscilla, who housed Paul (cf. Acts 18:3), could hardly have not noticed the provisions—food, clothing, perhaps some money (cf. Caragounis, "ὀψώνιον," p. 53)—that Silas and Timothy brought for Paul.

4. Among recent studies see esp. D. Georgi, *Die Gegner des Paulus im 2. Korintherbrief: Studien zur religiösen Propaganda in der Spätantike,* WMANT 11 (Neukirchen-Vluyn: Neukirchener, 1964), pp. 234-41; G. Dautzenberg, "Der Verzicht auf das apostolische Unterhaltsrecht: Eine exegetische Untersuchung zu 1 Kor 9," *Bib* 50 (1969): 212-32; C.K. Barrett, "Paul's Opponents in 2 Corinthians," *NTS* 17 (1970): 233-54; H.-D. Betz, *Der Apostel Paulus und die sokratische Tradition: Eine exegetische Untersuchung zu seiner 'Apologie' 2 Korinther 10-13,* BHTh 45 (Tübingen: Mohr, 1972), pp. 100-117; G. Theissen, "Legitimation und Lebensunterhalt: Ein Beitrag zur Soziologie urchristlicher Missionare," *NTS* 21 (1975): 192-221; and G. Agrell, *Work, Toil and Sustenance: An Examination of the View of Work in the New Testament, Taking into Consideration Views Found in Old Testament, Intertestamental and Early Rabbinic Writings* (Lund: Verbum-Håkan Ohlssons, 1976), pp. 106-15. For a concise description of the overall situation in Corinth, see W. G. Kümmel, *Introduction to the New Testament* (Nashville: Abingdon, 1975), pp. 271-75, 281-87.

5. See Georgi, *Gegner,* pp. 237, 239. Georgi, of course, views begging as typical not only of Cynics but of all Hellenistic missionaries—Jewish, pagan, and Christian (cf. *Gegner,* pp. 108-11, 188). See Theissen, "Lebensunterhalt," pp. 192, 204, 208, 210-11.

6. See Betz, *Apostel Paulus,* pp. 22-23, 25, 30, 39, 108-17.

7. Georgi, e.g., by viewing begging as typical of all missionaries (see above n. 5), thus has no alternative except to regard Paul's self-support as

most untypical, an alternative made credible by his insistence that Paul had a very personal and so distinctive apostolic self-understanding (cf. *Gegner,* pp. 40–41, esp. pp. 205–18). Barrett ("Opponents," p. 251) likewise assumes that Paul's opponents, and the Corinthians generally, were fundamentally influenced by Hellenistic culture, but not Paul. His apostleship and thereby his conduct as an apostle were fundamentally grounded in Christology. Cf. also C. K. Barrett, *A Commentary on the Second Epistle to the Corinthians,* HNTC (New York: Harper & Row, 1973), pp. 49, 282–84. This tendency to deny any significant contact between Paul and Hellenistic culture is all too typical of both conservative and liberal scholarship (so F.F. Bruce, *Paul: Apostle of the Heart Set Free* [Grand Rapids: Eerdmans, 1977], pp. 41, 75 (n. 3), 126–27, 142, 196 (n. 21), 238–43, 262; and G. Bornkamm, *Paul* [New York: Harper & Row, 1970], pp. 55–56, 64, 72, 75, 169–70, 188, 190, 223). Consequently, Betz's thesis that Paul was profoundly influenced by Socratic traditions (see *Apostel Paulus,* pp. 2–3, 14, 18, and passim) is all the more remarkable and commendable. Cf. also E. A. Judge, "St. Paul and Classical Society," *JAC* 15 (1972): 19–36.

8. Betz, e.g., too readily assumes that the aptness of Paul's choice of Socratic traditions to express and defend his practice of self-support and his apostleship in general is to be explained by their congruence with his Christology (cf. *Apostel Paulus,* pp. 51–57, 67, 79, 99–100). Theological considerations are not to be denied, but, as we shall see, sociological dimensions must also be recognized. Thus Theissen's appeal to social factors—politics, economics, ecology, and culture—in the debate over apostolic means of support (cf. "Lebensunterhalt," pp. 193–205) is to be welcomed, but his sociological argument is less helpful than it could be, since it is made at such a high level of generalization and is used more to explain the origin of the competing types of missionaries and their respective means of support than the dynamics of the conflict in Corinth.

9. See Musonius *frag.* 11 (pp. 80–84, Lutz).

10. See, e.g., Plato *Protag.* 349A; *Men.* 91D; Philostratus *V. Soph.* 494; and Diogenes Laertius, 9.50–52. Cf. further C. A. Forbes, *Teachers' Pay in Ancient Greece* (Lincoln: University of Nebraska, 1942), pp. 12–22.

11. See Xenophon *Anab.* 2.6.16; Philostratus *V. Soph.* 497 (Gorgias); Plato *Hipp. Major* 282E; Philostratus *V. Soph.* 495 (Hippias); *V. Soph.* 482, 496 (Prodicus); *V. Soph.* 499 (Antiphon); Plato *Euthyd.* 271A (Euthydemus); *Apol.* 20B (Evenus); and Isocrates *Antid.* 157, 224 (Isocrates).

12. Prodicus, e.g., charged fifty drachmas for attendance at his lecture in which he recited his famous story about Heracles' choice between virtue and vice (so Plato *Crat.* 384B; cf. Philostratus *V. Soph.* 482).

13. See Plato *Protag.* 328B, and Isocrates *Antid.* 155–56. Isocrates

(*Soph.* 3–9) criticized Sophists who were able to charge only three or four mina for their instruction.

14. See Forbes, *Teachers' Pay,* p. 14, n. 23.

15. The following Sophists are explicitly said to have charged fees: Scopelian (Philostratus *V. Soph.* 519), Lollianus (526–27), Polemo (538), Chrestus (591–92), Apollonius (600), Proclus (604), Domianus (605–6), and Heracleides (615).

16. On the second Sophistic, see now G. W. Bowersock, *Greek Sophists in the Roman Empire* (Oxford: Clarendon, 1969). Nicetes of Smyrna was a Sophist, contemporary with Paul (see Philostratus *V. Soph.* 512, and Bowersock, *Sophists,* p. 9, n. 1).

17. See Diogenes Laertius, 2.65, 72 (Aristippus), and 2.62 (Aeschines).

18. See Xenophon *Mem.* 1.2.60, and O. Gigon, *Kommentar zum ersten Buch von Xenophons Memorabilien* (Basel: Reinhardt, 1953), p. 90. On the matter of support in the history of Hellenistic philosophy and rhetoric, see the introductory essay of H. von Arnim's *Leben und Werke des Dio von Prusa* (Berlin: Weidmann, 1898), pp. 4–114.

19. On Zeno, Chrysippus, and Cleanthes charging fees, see Quintilian *Inst.* 12.7.9.

20. Plato himself rejected fees, but not so Speusippus (Diogenes Laertius, 4.2) and Xenocrates (4.8). It is not known whether Aristotle charged fees for instruction at the Lyceum, but he held that in principle philosophers could be paid (cf. Aristotle, *E. N.* 1164b 2–6).

21. Stoics of the early empire are often described as charging fees: Euphrates (so Apollonius *ep.* 51), Timocles (Lucian *J. Trag.* 27), Zenothemis (Lucian *Symp.* 32), and others (cf. Lucian *Herm.* 9; *Icar.* 5; and *Vit. auct.* 24–25).

22. See, e.g., Plato *Apol.* 19D–E, 31B–C, 33A–B; Xenophon *Mem.* 1.2.6–7, 61; 6.1–5, 11–14; *Apol.* 16, 26; and Diogenes Laertius, 2.27.

23. See esp. Plato *Protag.* 313C–D. For the motive of deceit, see Plato *Men.* 92A, and *Euthyd.* 277B; for that of greed, see Xenophon *Mem.* 1.2.7.

24. The label applied to Sophists (Philostratus *V. Soph.* 526) and to greedy philosophers (Philostratus *V. Apoll.* 1.13; Lucian *Nigr.* 25, and *Herm.* 59).

25. See Xenophon *Mem.* 1.2.5–6; 6.5; and Gigon *Kommentar,* pp. 34–35.

26. Xenophon *Apol.* 16.

27. See Xenophon *Mem.* 1.2.1, 5–6, 14, and Gigon *Kommentar,* 33–34.

28. See, e.g., ps.-Socrates *epp.* 1.2 (p. 218, 18–20, Malherbe); and 6.1–2 (p. 232, 5–19); and Lucian *Demon.* 4. Note also the depiction of the Platonic philosopher Nigrinus in Lucian *Nigr.* 25–26.

29. See, e.g., Philostratus *V. Soph.* 499, 519, 603.

30. See esp. Xenophon *Mem.* 1.6.2-3.

31. See, e.g., Plato *Protag.* 328B, 349A. Cf. also Plato *Men.* 91D, and Philostratus *V. Soph.* 494. The implication, that instruction offered free of charge was worth nothing, is made by Antiphon (so Xenophon *Mem.* 1.6.11-12).

32. See Lucian *Merc. cond.* 1-4.

33. See Diogenes Laertius, 3.9, 18-22.

34. See ibid., 5.1-4. The gifts are mentioned by Dio Chrysostom (*Orat.* 2.79).

35. The evidence is collected in my article "Simon the Shoemaker as an Ideal Cynic," *GRBS* 17 (1976): 41-53, esp. 45-46. Note that even the reclusive Epicurus permitted the wise man to pay court to a king, but only if in dire need (so Diogenes Laertius, 10.120).

36. On the philosophers in Augustus's household and the pattern he set for the principate, see G. W. Bowersock, *Augustus and the Greek World* (Oxford: Clarendon, 1965), pp. 30-41.

37. See Lucian *Philops.* 14.

38. See Lucian *Vit. auct.* 15 and 18. Cf. Epictetus *Diss.* 4.11.35.

39. See Philostratus *V. Soph.* 600.

40. See, e.g., Epictetus *Diss.* 4.1.177; Dio *Orat.* 77/78.34-36; and Lucian *Pisc.* 11-13.

41. See Diogenes Laertius, 2.25.

42. See, e.g., Seneca *De ben.* 5.6.2-7; Epictetus *frag.* 11 (p. 464, Schenkl); Dio *Orat.* 13.30; ps.-Socrates *ep.* 1 (pp. 218-26, Malherbe); and J. Sykutris, *Die Briefe des Sokrates und der Sokratiker* (Paderborn: Schöningh, 1933), pp. 13-26.

43. See, e.g., Diogenes Laertius, 6.25, 38, 58, and ps.-Diogenes *ep.* 46 (p. 176, Malherbe).

44. Ps.-Socrates *ep.* 8 (p. 244, 2-3, Malherbe).

45. See ibid., 9.1 (pp. 244, 22—246, 3, Malherbe).

46. See ibid., (p. 244, 27, Malherbe).

47. See ibid., 8 (p. 244, 10-11, Malherbe).

48. See Lucian *Vit. auct.* 12. Cf. further G. A. Gerhard, "Zur Legende vom Kyniker Diogenes," *ARW* 15 (1912): 388-408, esp. 390.

49. On the indignities suffered by philosophers at court, see also Diogenes Laertius, 2.67, 73, 78 (Aristippus); 3.18 (Plato): and 7.177 (Sphaerus). On the dangers involved in speaking with a philosopher's boldness ($\pi\alpha\rho\rho\eta\sigma\iota\alpha$), see my "Simon the Shoemaker," p. 46, n. 34.

50. See, e.g., ps.-Socrates *ep.* 9.2 (p. 246, 8-13, Malherbe).

51. See, e.g., the exchange of letters between King Antigonus and Zeno (Diogenes Laertius, 7.6-9).

52. On the theme of friendship between philosopher and king or patron, see, e.g., ps.-Socrates *ep.* 8 (p. 244, 5-7, Malherbe); Diogenes Laertius, 6.50; and esp. Lucian *Merc. cond.* 1, 3, 7, 20, and *Apol.* 9.

53. See Diogenes Laertius, 6.49, and ps.-Diogenes *ep.* 11 (p. 104, Malherbe). For other traditions of Diogenes begging, see Diogenes Laertius, 6.6, 38, 46, 56, 59, 60, 62, 67; ps.-Crates *ep.* 27 (p. 76, Malherbe); and ps.-Diogenes *ep.* 10 (pp. 102-4). Cf. further Gerhard, "Legende," pp. 397-99. Cynic tradition did not depict Diogenes' teacher Antisthenes as begging. Indeed, one tradition is critical of the practice (so Diogenes Laertius, 6.6). Antisthenes presumably supported himself by charging fees, if this conclusion may be read out of Diogenes Laertius, 6.4 and 9 (cf. also von Arnim, *Dio von Prusa,* p. 36). Thus Diogenes is credited with being the first Cynic to beg (so E. Zeller, *Die Philosophie der Griechen in ihrer geschichtlichen Entwicklung,* vol. 2, pt. 1, 5th ed. [Leipzig: Reisland, 1922], p. 317, n. 4).

54. See, e.g., Diogenes Laertius, 6.83 (Monimus) and 85-86 (Crates).

55. See ibid., 6.99.

56. See, e.g., Epictetus *Diss.* 3.22.10; Dio *Orat.* 32.9; Lucian *Fug.* 14, 17; *Pisc.* 35; *Tim.* 57; and Aulus Gellius *N. A.* 9.2.1-11.

57. See, e.g., Diogenes Laertius, 6.38, 50, and Gerhard, "Legende," pp. 397-98. Cf. further von Arnim, *Dio von Prusa,* pp. 37-40.

58. For Diogenes living in public buildings, see, e.g., Teles *frag.* II (p. 8, 40-41, O'Neil); Dio *Orat.* 4.12-13; 6.14; Diogenes Laertius, 6.23, 64 (temples); Teles *frag.* II—p. 8, 40-41—(baths); Diogenes Laertius, 6.22 (stoas); Dio *Orat.* 6.14; 8.4-5; and 9.4 (gymnasia). For Crates and Hipparchia living together in the stoas, see Musonius *frag.* 14 (p. 92, 1-4, Lutz). For Metrocles in a workshop, see Teles *frag.* IV^A (p. 42, 124-27). More generally, see Epictetus, 3.22.16; Lucian *Vit. auct.* 9; and Zeller, *Philosophie der Griechen,* vol. 2, pt. 1, p. 317, n. 5. Many people besides Cynics had no home or apartment and so had to live wherever they could (see B. W. Frier, "The Rental Market in Early Imperial Rome," *JRS* 67 [1977]: 27-37, esp. 30, n. 20).

59. See, e.g., Epictetus *Diss.* 3.22.10.

60. See, e.g., ps.-Crates *ep.* 22 (p. 72, Malherbe), and Diogenes Laertius, 6.67.

61. On Cynics being refused, see, e.g., Diogenes Laertius, 6.6, 56; 7.17.

62. On begging as shameful, see, e.g., ps.-Crates *ep.* 17 (p. 66, Malherbe), and ps.-Diogenes *ep.* 34 (pp. 142-44).

63. See, e.g., Menippus, who is said to have become wealthy from begging (so Diogenes Laertius, 6.99) and several other Cynics whose wallets contained gold (so Lucian *Pisc.* 45, and *Peregr.* 30; cf. *Fug.* 20). For criticisms of Cynic begging, see Seneca *De ben.* 2.17.1-2; Epictetus *Diss.* 3.22.50; and Lucian *Pisc.* 29-37, 40-42, 47-52; and *Fug.* 30-31.

64. See, e.g., Diogenes Laertius, 6.37, 72, and esp. ps.-Crates *ep.* 26 (p. 76, Malherbe).

65. So, e.g., Demonax (cf. Lucian *Demon.* 4, 8, 63), and Dio Chrysostom (cf. *Orat.* 3.15).

66. See pp. 39–40.

67. See Diogenes Laertius, 7.168–70. Cf. also Seneca *ep.* 44.3; Epictetus *Diss.* 3.26.23; and Plutarch *De vit. aere al.* 830C–D.

68. See Athenaeus *Deipnos.* 4.168A. Cf. Diogenes Laertius, 2.125.

69. See Philostratus *V. Soph.* 488.

70. See Lucian *Tox.* 31.

71. See Musonius *frag.* 11 (p. 82, 22–33, Lutz).

72. See, e.g., ps.-Socrates *epp.* 9.4 (p. 246, 29–33, Malherbe); 11 (p. 248, 18–19); and 13.1 (p. 250, 26–27). For what follows, see also my article "Simon the Shoemaker," pp. 43–53.

73. See ps.-Socrates *ep.* 18.2 (p. 266, 21–16, Malherbe).

74. See ibid., 8 (p. 244, 4, Malherbe).

75. See Teles, *frag.* IV^B (p. 48, 21–50, 32, O'Neil).

76. See esp. Lucian *Vit. auct.* 7 and 11, where tanners, carpenters, and the like are deemed suited to Cynic philosophy. Cf. also Lucian *Merc. cond.* 6; *Tim.* 7; and Plutarch *Maxime cum princ. phil. diss.* 776B.

77. See esp. Musonius *frag.* 11 (p. 82, 6–8, Lutz).

78. See ibid. (p. 80, 10-12, Lutz) and A. C. van Geytenbeek, *Musonius Rufus and Greek Diatribe* (Assen: Van Gorcum, 1963), p. 129.

79. On these aspects of the tractate, see, e.g., van Geytenbeek, *Musonius Rufus,* pp. 131–34, and R. MacMullen, *Roman Social Relations 50 B.C. to A.D. 284* (New Haven: Yale, 1974), pp. 29–30.

80. Musonius *frag.* 11 (p. 82, 30–31, Lutz—her translation).

81. Ibid. (p. 82, 12–13, Lutz—my translation).

82. See ibid. (p. 82, 31–33, Lutz).

83. Note the report that Musonius refused to accept anything from a Syrian king who had visited the philosopher (so Musonius *frag.* 8 [p. 66, 26–31, Lutz]).

84. See ibid., 11 (p. 82, 2–4, Lutz).

85. See ibid., 3 (p. 42, 28–29, Lutz); cf. *frag.* 4 (p. 46, 13–27).

86. See Teles *frag.* IV^B (p. 48, 27–28, O'Neil).

87. See esp. ps.-Socrates *ep.* 13.1 (p. 250, 18–27, Malherbe).

88. Musonius *frag.* 11 (p. 82, 22–24, Lutz—her translation).

89. On what follows, see also my "Simon the Shoemaker," pp. 49–53.

90. See ps.-Socrates *ep.* 12 (p. 250, 3–7, Malherbe).

91. See ibid., 13.1-2 (pp. 250, 27—252, 9, Malherbe). Ridicule of the wisdom of artisan-philosophers is found also in ps.-Socrates *ep.* 9.4 (p. 246, 29–33). Cf. also Epictetus *Diss.* 1.19.16–23, and Lucian *Fug.* 12–13, and *Vit. auct.* 11.

92. See, e.g., H. Conzelmann, *1 Corinthians,* Hermeneia (Philadelphia: Fortress, 1975) p. 54.

93. See, e.g., Lightfoot, *Epistles of St. Paul,* p. 172, and Bruce, *Paul,* p. 248.

94. See Betz, *Apostel Paulus,* pp. 44–57.

95. Cf. the description of a rhetor in Lucian *Somn.* 13.

96. See Betz, *Apostel Paulus,* pp. 55–57. So also Conzelmann, *1 Corinthians,* p. 54.

97. See p. 35. The sociological dimension of this language in 1 Corinthians has been emphasized by G. Theissen, "Soziale Schichtung in der korinthischen Gemeinde: Ein Beitrag zur Soziologie des hellenistischen Urchristentums," *ZNW* 65 (1974): 232–72, esp. 233–35.

98. See Lucian *Cat.* 1, 14–15, 20, and 22. Cf. also the description of the sculptor in his *Somnium* (esp. 6–9 and 13).

99. See Lucian *Somn.* 13, and above p. 35.

100. This point is emphasized also by Theissen, "Lebensunterhalt," p. 204. Cf. Agrell, *Work,* p. 108.

101. On the paradigmatic function of 1 Corinthians 9, see esp. Dungan, *Churches of Paul,* pp. 4–6, 21–22, 33. Cf. also Dautzenberg, "Verzicht," p. 213, and Agrell, *Work,* p. 106. This function renders invalid attempts to lift this chapter out of its literary context, as do J. Weiss, *Der erste Korintherbrief,* MeyerK 5, 9th ed. (Göttingen: Vandenhoeck & Ruprecht, 1910), pp. xl–xli, and W. Schmithals, "Die Korintherbriefe als Briefsammlung," *ZNW* 64 (1973): 263–88.

102. On understanding the ταῦτα of verse 15a as referring to the arguments cited in verses 7–14 rather than to the rights in verses 4–6, see Dungan, *Churches of Paul,* p. 21, n. 2.

103. This reading of verse 19 takes the conjunction γάρ ("for") as inferential (so BAG 151b) rather than as merely resumptive (so, e.g., H. Lietzmann and W. G. Kümmel, *An die Korinther I–II* HNT 9, 4th ed. [Tübingen: Mohr, 1949], p. 43, and Conzelmann, *1 Corinthians,* p. 158, n. 1).

104. For details, see pp. 53, 54–55, and 57.

105. See further my article, "Paul's Tentmaking and the Problem of His Social Class," *JBL* 97 (1978): 555–64.

106. For details, see pp. 54–55.

107. See pp. 47–49.

108. That the "necessity" refers to Paul's divine commission to preach is pointed out by many: Weiss, *Erster Korintherbrief,* p. 240; P. Bachmann, *Der erste Brief des Paulus an die Korinther,* KNT 7, 4th ed. (Leipzig and Erlangen: Deichert, 1936), p. 328; and Conzelmann, *1 Corinthians,* p. 158, n. 26. On the use of this notion for apostolic self-understanding, see K. Deissner, "Das Sendungsbewusstseins der Urchristenheit," *ZST* 7 (1930): 772–90.

109. This is the linear force of the present subjunctive εὐαγγελίζωμαι. Contrast the punctiliar force of the following aorist subjunctive εὐαγγελίσωμαι. Cf. also the discussion in G. Zuntz, *The Text of the*

Epistles (London: Oxford, 1953), p. 110.

110. The finality of Paul's decision is expressed by the perfect κέχρημαι (so, e.g., Conzelmann, *1 Corinthians,* p. 157).

111. On Paul's boasting, see the fine discussion in Agrell, *Work,* pp. 112-13.

112. On philosophers teaching "free of charge," see, e.g., Xenophon *Mem.* 1.2.60-61; Musonius *frag.* 8 (p. 66, 26-31, Lutz); Apollonius *ep.* 2; Dio *Orat.* 3.15; 35.1; and Lucian *Nigr.* 25-26.

113. 1 Cor. 9:17-18 is notoriously difficult to interpret. Not even the punctuation of verses 17b-18 is sure, though the punctuation of the Nestle text is probably right (see Weiss, *Erster Korintherbrief,* pp. 240-41). In addition, commentators are divided over whether the condition in verse 17a or verse 17b is the actual condition of Paul, with the majority preferring verse 17b, i.e., Paul's preaching the gospel "unwillingly" (ἄκων); e.g., Bachmann, *Erster Brief,* pp. 328-31; Lietzmann and Kümmel, *An die Korinther,* p. 43; and Conzelmann, *1 Corinthians,* p. 158. And yet, this view fails to maintain that Paul *was entitled* to a "salary" (cf. v. 6), which is the point of verse 17a (and v. 18). Verse 17a is thus Paul's actual situation: He accepted the "necessity" of his having to preach "willingly" (ἐκών). Verse 17b is purely hypothetical.

114. It is customary to view Paul's choice of κερδαίνειν as reflecting rabbinic usage (so D. Daube, "Κερδαίνω as a Missionary Term," *HTR* 40 [1947]: 109-20, followed by Lietzmann and Kümmel, *An die Korinther,* p. 180; C. K. Barrett, *A Commentary on the First Epistle to the Corinthians,* HNTC [New York: Harper & Row, 1968], p. 211; and Conzelmann, *1 Corinthians,* p. 159, n. 17). But none of the rabbinic parallels adduced by Daube is found in discussions of support. Rather, Paul here is dependent, as he has been throughout 1 Corinthians 9, on philosophical discussions of support, as is clear from the use of κερδαίνειν in Xenophon *Mem.* 1.2.7; Epictetus *Diss.* 4.1.177; Dio *Orat.* 70.5; ps.-Diogenes *ep.* 29.3 (p. 126, 23-26, Malherbe); and Philostratus *V. Apoll.* 8.7.3.

115. See the concise summary of the situation in Kümmel, *Introduction,* pp. 281-87.

116. See p. 55.

117. See also 1 Thess. 2:7-11 and above p. 48.

118. This interpretation takes both purpose clauses in verse 12 to be dependent on "what I do I shall also continue to do," rather than only the first clause, with the second taken with the preceding participle (θελόντων) (so most commentators: A. Plummer, *A Critical and Exegetical Commentary on the Second Epistle of Paul to the Corinthians,* ICC [Edinburgh: Clark, 1915], pp. 307-8; H. Windisch, *Der zweite Korintherbrief,* MeyerK 6, 9th ed. [Göttingen: Vandenhoeck & Ruprecht, 1924], pp. 339-40; Lietzmann and Kümmel, *An die Korinther,* pp. 148, 210-11; and

Barrett, *Second Corinthians*, pp. 284–85). This interpretation, however, not only breaks up the parallelism of the verse but also makes Paul react too much in terms of the purposes of the opponents. On the contrary, it was Paul's purpose that the opponents change their position regarding support; otherwise, they would be false apostles (v. 13).

119. This point has been made many times (see esp. Windisch, *Zweiter Korintherbrief,* pp. 100–101).

120. See p. 93, n.2.

121. So also Plummer, *Second Epistle to the Corinthians,* p. 302; Windisch, *Zweiter Korintherbrief,* p. 334; and P. E. Hughes, *Paul's Second Epistle to the Corinthians,* NICNT (Grand Rapids: Eerdmans, 1962), p. 384.

122. See Lucian *Somn.* 13. Cf. also Aristotle *Pol.* 1337b 14–15; Athenaeus *Deipnos.* 12.512B; Seneca *ep.* 47.10; Plutarch *De fort.* 318C; and Lucian *Somn.* 9.

123. See Lucian *Merc. cond.* 22. Cf. also Diogenes Laertius, 7.15.

124. So, e.g., Plummer, *Second Epistle to the Corinthians,* p. 303, and Barrett, *Second Corinthians,* p. 282. Windisch *(Zweiter Korintherbrief,* pp. 334–35) rejects this approach and hints at the social connotation of this word.

125. See pp. 34–35. That the toils (κόποι) referred to here include Paul's toils as a tentmaker is argued, e.g., by Barrett, *Second Corinthians,* p. 186.

126. See p. 35. That the sleeplessness, hunger, etc., referred to here were a consequence of Paul's plying a trade is argued, e.g., by Windisch, *Zweiter Korintherbrief,* p. 205.

127. Barrett (*Second Corinthians,* p. 190) rightly recognizes here another indirect reference to Paul's life as an artisan.

128. Commentators (esp. Windisch, *Zweiter Korintherbrief,* p. 400) see here a reference to Paul's working at a trade, but they do not emphasize the physical "expense" Paul expected to have to absorb by doing such work.

129. See p. 37.

Selected Bibliography

Agrell, G. *Work, Toil and Sustenance: An Examination of the View of Work in the New Testament: Taking into Consideration Views Found in the Old Testament, Intertestamental and Early Rabbinic Writings.* Lund: Verbum Håkan Ohlssons, 1976.

Arnim, H. von. *Leben und Werke des Dio von Prusa.* Berlin: Weidmann, 1898.

Baldry, H. C. "Zeno's Ideal State," *JHS* 79 (1959): 3–25.

Barrett, C. K. "Paul's Opponents in 2 Corinthians," *NTS* 17 (1970): 233–54.

Baur, F. C. *Paul the Apostle of Jesus Christ: His Life and Work, His Epistles and Doctrine.* 2 vols. London: Williams & Norgate, 1876.

Betz, H.-D. *Der Apostel Paulus und die sokratische Tradition: Eine exegetische Untersuchung zu seiner 'Apologie' 2 Korinther 10–13.* BHTh 45. Tübingen: Mohr, 1972.

Bienert, W. *Die Arbeit nach der Lehre der Bibel: Eine Grundlegung evangelischer Sozialethik.* Stuttgart: Evangelisches Verlagswerk GMBH, 1954.

Biscottini, M. "L'Archivio di Tryphon tesstitore di Oxyrhynchos," *Aegyptus* 46 (1966): 60–90, 186–292.

Blümner, H. *Technologie und Terminologie der Gewerbe und Künste bei Griechen und Römern.* 4 vols. Leipzig and Berlin: Teubner, 1875–78. Vol. 1, 2d ed., 1912.

Bornkamm, G. *Paul.* New York: Harper & Row, 1971.

Bousset, W. *Kyrios Christos: A History of the Belief in Christ from the Beginnings of Christianity to Irenaeus.* Nashville: Abingdon, 1970.

Bowersock, G. W. *Augustus and the Greek World.* Oxford: Clarendon, 1965.

———. *Greek Sophists in the Roman Empire.* Oxford: Clarendon, 1969.

Brewster, E. "In Roman Egypt," *CW* 29 (1935): 25–29.

———. "A Weaver of Oxyrhynchus," *TAPA* 58 (1927): 132–54.

Bruce, F. F. *Paul: Apostle of the Heart Set Free*. Grand Rapids: Eerdmans, 1977.

Brunt, P.A. "Aspects of the Social Thought of Dio Chrysostom and of the Stoics," *PCPhS* 19 (1973): 9–34.

Bultmann, R. *Theology of the New Testament*. 2 vols. New York: Scribner's, 1951, 1955.

Burchard, C. *Der dreizehnte Zeuge: Traditions- und kompositionsgeschichtliche Untersuchungen zu Lukas Darstellung der Früzeit des Paulus*. FRLANT 103. Göttingen: Vandenhoeck & Ruprecht, 1970.

Burford, A. *Craftsmen in Greek and Roman Society*. London: Thames & Hudson, 1972.

Cadbury, H. J. "Lexical Notes on Luke-Acts III: Luke's Interest in Lodging," *JBL* 45 (1926): 305–22.

Casson, L. "The Athenian Upper Classes and New Comedy," *TAPA* 106 (1976): 29–59.

———. *Travel in the Ancient World*. Toronto: Hakkert, 1974.

Caragounis, G. "Ὀψώνιον: A Reconsideration of Its Meaning," *NovT* 16 (1974): 35–57.

Daube, D. "Κερδαίνω as a Missionary Term," *HTR* 40 (1947): 109–20.

Dautzenberg, G. "Der Verzicht auf das apostolische Unterhaltsrecht: Eine exegetische Untersuchung zu 1 Kor 9," *Bib* 50 (1969): 212–32.

Deissmann, A. *Light from the Ancient East*. London: Hodder & Stoughton, 1927.

———. *Paul: A Study in Social and Religious History*. London: Hodder & Stoughton, 1926.

Deissner, K. "Das Sendungsbewussteins der Urchristenheit," *ZST* 7 (1930): 772–90.

Dudley, D. R. *A History of Cynicism from Diogenes to the Sixth Century A.D.* London: Methuen, 1937.

Dungan, D. L. *The Sayings of Jesus in the Churches of Paul: The Use of the Synoptic Tradition in the Regulation of Early Church Life*. Philadelphia: Fortress, 1971.

Dupont, J. *Le Discours de Milet: Testament Pastoral de Saint Paul (Actes 20:18–36)*. Paris: Les Editions au Cerf, 1962.

Enslin, M. "Paul and Gamaliel," *JR* 7 (1927): 360–75.

Finley, M. I. *The Ancient Economy*. Berkeley: University of California, 1973.

Forbes, C. A. "Expanded Uses of the Greek Gymnasium," *CPh* 40 (1945): 32–42.

———. *Teachers' Pay in Ancient Greece*. Lincoln: University of Nebraska, 1942.

Forbes, R. J. *Studies in Ancient Technology*. 9 vols. to date. Leiden: Brill, 1955–

Frank, T., ed. *An Economic Survey of Ancient Rome*. 6 vols. Baltimore: Johns Hopkins, 1933–40.

Frier, B. "The Rental Market in Early Imperial Rome," *JRS* 67 (1977) 27–37.

Geoghegan, A. T. *The Attitude towards Labor in Early Christianity and Ancient Culture*. Washington, D.C.: Catholic University of America, 1945.

Georgi, D. *Die Gegner des Paulus im 2. Korintherbrief: Studien zum religiösen Propaganda in der Spätantike*. WMANT 11. Neukirchen-Vluyn: Neukirchener, 1964.

Gerhard, G. "Zur Legende vom Kyniker Diogenes," *ARW* 15 (1912): 388–408.

Geytenbeek, A. C. van. *Musonius Rufus and Greek Diatribe*. Assen: Van Gorcum, 1963.

Gigon, O. *Kommentar zum ersten Buch von Xenophons Memorabilien*. Basel: Reinhardt, 1953.

Hansack, E. "Er lebte . . . von seinem eigenen Einkommen (Apg. 28:30)," *BZ* 19 (1975): 249–53.

———. "Nochmals zu Apostelgeschichte 28:30," *BZ* 21 (1977): 118–21.

Hauck, F. *Die Stellung des Urchristentums zu Arbeit und Geld*. BFCT 2, 3. Gütersloh: Bertelsmann, 1921.

Heinrici, G. "Zur Geschichte der Anfänge paulinischer Gemeinden," *ZWT* 20 (1877): 89–129.

Herrmann, J. "Vertragsinhalt und Rechtsnatur der διδασκαλικαί," *JJP* 11–12 (1957–58): 119–39.

Hock, R. F. "Paul's Tentmaking and the Problem of His Social Class," *JBL* 97 (1978): 555–64.

———. "Simon the Shoemaker as an Ideal Cynic," *GRBS* 17 (1976): 41–53.

Holzapfel, H. *Die sittliche Wertung der körperlichen Arbeit im christlichen Altertum*. Würzburg: Rita, 1941.

Jeremias, J. "Zöllner und Sünder," *ZNW* 30 (1931): 293–300.

Jervell, J. *Luke and the People of God*. Minneapolis: Augsburg, 1972.

Judge, E. A. "St. Paul and Classical Society," *JAC* 15 (1972): 19–36.

Kalischer, S. "Die Wertschätzung der Arbeit in Bibel und Talmud," *Judaica: Festschrift zu H. Cohens siebzigstem Geburtstag*, pp. 580–98. Berlin: Cassirer, 1912.

Kienast, D. "Ein vernachlässigtes Zeugnis für die Reichpolitik Trajans: Die zweite tarsische Rede des Dion von Prusa," *Historia* 20 (1971): 62–80.

Kreissig, H. "Zur sozialen Zusammensetzung der früchristlichen Gemeinde im ersten Jahrhundert u. Z.," *Eirene* 6 (1967): 91–100.

Kümmel, W. G. *Introduction to the New Testament*. Nashville: Abingdon, 1975.

———. *The New Testament: The History of the Investigation of Its Problems.* Nashville: Abingdon, 1972.

Lau, O. *Schuster und Schusterhandwerk in der griechisch-römischen Literatur und Kunst.* Dissertation, Bonn, 1967.

Laub, F. *Eschatologische Verkündigung und Lebensgestaltung: Eine Untersuchung zum Wirken des Apostels beim Aufbau der Gemeinde in Thessalonike.* Regensburg: Pustet, 1973.

Lynch, J. P. *Aristotle's School: A Study of a Greek Educational Institution.* Berkeley: University of California, 1972.

McIntyre, J. and Richmond, I. A. "Tents of the Roman Army and Leather from Birdoswald," *TCWA* 34 (1934): 62–90.

MacMullen, R. *Enemies of the Roman Order: Treason, Unrest and Alienation in the Empire.* Cambridge: Harvard, 1966.

———. *Roman Social Relations 50 B.C. to A.D. 284.* New Haven: Yale, 1974.

Malherbe, A. J. "Gentle as a Nurse: The Cynic Background of 1 Thess. 2," *NovT* 12 (1970): 203–17.

———. "The Inhospitality of Diotrephes," *God's Christ and His People: Studies in Honour of N. A. Dahl,* edited by J. Jervell and W. Meeks, pp. 222-32. Oslo: Universitets-forlaget, 1977.

———. *Social Aspects of Early Christianity.* Baton Rouge: Louisiana State University, 1977.

Metzger, B. M. *A Textual Commentary on the Greek New Testament.* London: United Bible Societies, 1971.

Meyer, S. *Arbeit und Handwerk im Talmud.* Berlin: Benzian, 1878.

Michaelis, W. "Σκηνοποιός," *TDNT* 7 (1971): 393–94.

Nestle, E. "The Aprons and Handkerchiefs of St. Paul," *ExpT* 13 (1901-1902): 282.

———. "St. Paul's Handicraft (Acts 18:3)," *JBL* 11 (1892): 205–6.

Neusner, J. *The Rabbinic Traditions about the Pharisees before 70.* 3 vols. Leiden: Brill, 1971.

Nock, A. D. *St. Paul.* New York: Harper & Row, 1963.

Packer, J. "Housing and Population in Imperial Ostia and Rome," *JRS* 57 (1967): 80–95.

Plumptre, E. "St. Paul as a Man of Business," *Expositor* 1 (1875): 259–66.

Rabinowitz, W. G. *Aristotle's 'Protrepticus' and the Sources of Its Reconstruction.* Berkeley: University of California, 1957.

Ramsay, W. "Roads and Travel (in the NT)," *HDB* 5 (1904): 375–402.

———. *St. Paul the Traveller and Roman Citizen.* New York: Putnam's Sons, 1904.

Safrai, S. and M. Stern, eds. *The Jewish People in the First Century.* 2 vols. to date. Philadelphia: Fortress, 1974–

Saum, F. "Apostelgeschichte 28:30," *BZ* 20 (1976): 226–29.

Schmithals, W. "Die Korintherbriefe als Briefsammlung," *ZNW* 64 (1973): 263–88.

———. *Paul and the Gnostics.* Nashville: Abingdon, 1972.

Silva, R. "Eran, pues, de oficio, fabricantes de tiendas," *EstBib* 24 (1965): 123–34.

Soares, T. G. "Paul's Missionary Methods," *BW* 34 (1909): 326–36.

Sykutris, J. *Die Briefe des Sokrates und der Sokratiker.* Paderborn: Schönigh, 1933.

Theissen, G. "Legitimation und Lebensunterhalt: Ein Beitrag zu Soziologie urchristlicher Missionare," *NTS* 21 (1975): 192–221.

———. "Soziale Schichtung in der korinthischen Gemeinde: Ein Beitrag zur Soziologie des hellenistischen Urchristentums," *ZNW* 65 (1974): 232–72.

Thompson, D. B. "The House of Simon the Shoemaker," *Archaeology* 13 (1960): 234–40.

Travlos, J. *Pictorial Dictionary of Ancient Athens.* New York: Prager, 1971.

Urbach, E. E. "Class-Status and Leadership in the World of the Palestinian Sages," *Proceedings of the Israel Academy of Sciences and Humanities,* vol. 2, pp. 38–74. Jerusalem: Central, 1968.

Webster, G. *The Roman Imperial Army of the First and Second Centuries A.D.* New York: Funk & Wagnalls, 1969.

Weizsäcker, C. von. *The Apostolic Age of the Christian Church.* 2 vols. London: Williams & Norgate, 1897.

Westermann, W. L. "Apprentice Contracts and the Apprentice System in Roman Egypt," *CPh* 9 (1914): 295–315.

Williams, C. S. C. *Alterations to the Text of the Synoptic Gospels and Acts.* Oxford: Blackwell, 1951.

Wycherley, R. E. "The Garden of Epicurus," *Phoenix* 13 (1959): 73–77.

———. "The Painted Stoa," *Phoenix* 7 (1953): 20–35.

———. "Peripatos: The Athenian Philosophical Scene: Parts I & II," *G & R* 8 (1961): 152–63 and 9 (1962): 2–21.

Zambon, A. "Διδασκαλικαί," *Aegyptus* 15 (1935): 3–66.

Zeller, E. *Die Philosophie der Griechen in ihrer geschichtlichen Entwicklung.* 6 vols. 5th ed. Leipzig: Reisland, 1922.

Zuntz, G. *The Text of the Epistles.* London: Oxford, 1953.

Index of Ancient Sources

NEW TESTAMENT

107

OTHER ANCIENT SOURCES

(Editions used of authors listed below, unless otherwise specified, are those of the Loeb Classical Library.)